Picture
Books
for Children

Mary Northrup

Picture Books

for Children

Fiction, Folktales, and Poetry

American Library Association
Chicago | 2012

MARY NORTHRUP is the reference librarian at Metropolitan Community College–Maple Woods, Kansas City, Missouri. She has written for children, teachers, librarians, and writers. Her publication credits include several chapters in *Writing and Publishing: The Librarians' Handbook* (American Library Association, 2010) and the books *Short on Time, Long on Learning* (Linworth, 2000) and *American Computer Pioneers* (Enslow, 1998). She has written for Writer's Institute Publications, including four editions of *Writer's Guide to Current Children's Books*, and is a frequent contributor to its annual *Children's Writer Guide*. She reviews for *LMC: Library Media Connection* and *EMRO: Educational Media Reviews Online*. Her articles have appeared in *Book Links*, *Children's Writer*, and other publications. Northrup earned her master's degree in library science at the University of Wisconsin–Milwaukee. Her undergraduate degree is in elementary education. She serves on the board of the Missouri Center for the Book.

Printed in the United States of America
16 15 14 13 12   5 4 3 2 1

Extensive effort has gone into ensuring the reliability of the information in this book; however, the publisher makes no warranty, express or implied, with respect to the material contained herein.

ISBNs: 978-0-8389-1144-0 (paper); 978-0-8389-9439-9 (PDF); 978-0-8389-9460-3 (ePub); 978-0-8389-9461-0 (Kindle). For more information on digital formats, visit the ALA Store at alastore.ala.org and select eEditions.

LIBRARY OF CONGRESS CATALOGING-IN-PUBLICATION DATA
Northrup, Mary.
  Picture books for children : fiction, folktales, and poetry / Mary Northrup.
—Fifth edition.
     p. cm
  Revised edition of: Picture books for children / Patricia J. Cianciolo.
Fourth edition. 1997.
  Includes bibliographical references and index.
  ISBN 978-0-8389-1144-0 (alk. paper)
  1. Picture books for children—Bibliography. 2. Illustrated children's books—Bibliography. 3. Children—Books and reading—United States. I. Cianciolo, Patricia J. Picture books for children. II. Title.
  Z1037.C565 2012
  011.62—dc23
                                                                2011044734

Book design in Minion Pro and Alan Font by Casey Bayer. Cover image © xgw1028/Shutterstock, Inc.

♾ This paper meets the requirements of ANSI/NISO Z39.48–1992 (Permanence of Paper).

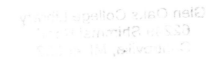

To Mom and Dad,
who encouraged my love of reading and learning

Contents

Preface

The purpose of this book is to present some of the best of children's picture books for use in the classroom, library, or home. What an enjoyable experience it was to select, reading or rereading many picture books, experiencing the beauty of the words and the art.

The scope of the book includes fiction, poetry, and folktales/fairy tales. Nonfiction or informational picture books are not included, although fictionalized versions of historical events and lives are. If there was any doubt, I checked the Cataloging-in-Publication data and noted the Library of Congress subject headings to ensure that "Juvenile Fiction" was the subheading.

The books are intended for four- to eight-year-olds, although some indicate a younger or older age. Age designations, like reading levels, are guidelines only. Your child or class may enjoy certain of the books at age three, or ten, or older.

The selected books were in print as of the writing and span the years from 2000 to 2011, with the majority published in the last five years. The books are hardcover, unless specified as available only in paperback or library binding.

The audience for this book includes K–3 teachers, librarians in schools and public libraries, preservice teachers and librarians taking children's literature courses, day care center teachers, parents and grandparents, homeschooling parents, other caregivers, and writers and aspiring writers who are interested in picture books. I hope that those in this audience will find the annotations helpful in selecting quality books for programming, classroom use, one-on-one sharing, and inspiration for books of the future.

I selected books from the very many I read to show the wide variety of styles in art and in story, to feature a broad range of authors and illustrators, to portray worldwide diversity, to provide a balance of female and male main characters, and to show the many subjects in picture books written to engage children. I included some of the books that have won awards that recognize excellence in picture books, including the Caldecott Medal, the Coretta Scott King Book Award, the Schneider Family Book Award, the Pura Belpré Award, the Boston Globe–Horn Book Award, the Christopher Award, the Charlotte Zolotow Award, the Golden Kite Award, the Sydney Taylor Book Award, and the Américas Book Award. Books published in Canada are included, as well as books written for children in foreign countries—Japan, France, Germany, and others—before appearing in the United States.

Several alphabet books fall within the scope of this book. A classic subgenre of picture books, the best ones are clever, beautiful, surprising, or all of these. Some, such as Gennady Spirin's *A Apple Pie*, are classic. Others, like Yuyi Morales's *Just in Case*, feature an alphabet within the story.

I included poetry, although it is not strictly defined as fiction. Several of the books that feature poems, such as *Oh, Brother!* by Nikki Grimes, could also be considered fiction because they tell a story with a beginning, middle, and end and develop their characters. Quality picture books classified as poetry will, besides offering a pleasurable listening experience, aid in the appreciation of language which helps the child developing reading and writing skills.

Folktales, fairy tales, and other stories based on the oral traditions or traditional literature of countries are a natural for picture books. This book contains one chapter devoted to these. I included a variety of types of tales, including tales from other countries and cultures.

It is my hope that the readers of this book will find many titles to read to children and to select for, or borrow from, the library. Teachers and librarians, of course, know the value of libraries and the importance of support for public libraries and school libraries. Aspiring writers must read to learn their craft and so are usually big library supporters. Parents and caregivers in the know realize what a treasure their libraries are.

Might I also include a plea to support your independent bookstore when you purchase books for your own personal library? These local businesses make our cities unique and culturally vibrant. And if your city is home to a children's bookstore, so much the better! Here in Kansas City, Missouri, we are fortunate to have the Reading Reptile, a treasure for the region.

A hearty thank-you goes to the Mid-Continent Public Library, whose employees at my local branch and throughout the system helped with a constant stream of interlibrary loan books. I could not have written this book without you.

Thank you, too, to the librarians and teachers who talked to me about books. It is always a pleasure to discuss picture books with professionals and to trade suggestions of favorites.

Preface

I would like to thank my editor at ALA Editions, Stephanie Zvirin. She is a joy to work with and is unfailingly upbeat and encouraging, no matter how many questions I ask. I must also thank Patricia J. Cianciolo, the author of four previous editions of *Picture Books for Children* published by the American Library Association, who paved the way for this book. Her books were a guidepost and an inspiration to me. And finally, my deep appreciation goes to Crockett Johnson, author of *Harold and the Purple Crayon,* and Maj Lindman, author of the Flicka, Ricka, Dicka books. These are my earliest memories of picture books, and among my favorite books as a child. From these and other books in the children's section of the public library I learned to love books and reading, school and learning, and, eventually, teaching and writing. Like all good picture books, their work lives on.

The Picture Book

Where Words and Art Come Together

Open a book and enter a new world. Open a picture book and enter that world magnified, through words and illustrations. The text and art in the picture book intertwine so completely that, in the best, we cannot imagine one without the other.

Think of the books that you remember from your childhood. Perhaps a classic, such as *Make Way for Ducklings* or *The Little Engine that Could,* or a character, such as Frances, Mike Mulligan, Curious George, or Madeline. Being read to and visiting a library, thrilled by the prospect of finding shelves full of choices, may be cherished memories. It is these moments that we, as librarians, teachers, and parents, wish for the children to whom we read and for whom we provide books.

Picture books encompass all subjects, fiction or nonfiction. Not just for the prereading crowd, they entertain and entrance the youngest children to adults. Their reach is far, and their power to inspire is wide. In this chapter we examine the picture book, its elements and structure, its uses and its future.

WHAT IS A PICTURE BOOK?

With a small number of pages, and not too many words on each page, picture books appear to be the easiest children's books—to read, to write, to analyze. But this perceived simplicity belies a complex art form. As in a poem, a genre to which the picture book has been compared, each word must count. The structure is rigid. Most important, the words and illustrations must work together: one supports and builds on the other, and even transforms it. The author of a picture book writes the text always mindful of how those words will be illustrated. The illustrator creates the art to integrate completely with the text.

A picture book usually contains thirty-two pages but can be longer or shorter, always in increments of eight pages. This standard came about because of the way pages are printed and bound. Of these thirty-two pages, twenty-eight or twenty-nine make up the story. The others include the title page, copyright page, and sometimes a dedication page or a double page for the title. Usually, then, the book contains fourteen double pages. Each page or two-page spread holds the words and illustrations that create one scene of the story. The page breaks supply a natural pause at the end of the words on that page. Page turns reveal a new scene of picture and text, and the story continues.

The number of words in a picture book is fewer than 1,000, and often considerably under that. Books that contain much longer text in relation to the illustrations are considered illustrated books rather than picture books. In these, one scene is portrayed on a page spread, out of several described in the accompanying text.

In the picture book, placement of the text and illustrations in relation to each other influences the pacing and mood of the story. Variations range from text and art separated, either on different pages or in a box or border on the same page, to both integrated on the same page, either as blocks of text within the illustration or in nonstandard form such as swirls or lines. In some, the words even become part of the illustration because of their form and shape.

How the illustrations and the text work with each other—that is the essence of the picture book. In some cases, the illustrations portray what the text indicates. In others, the illustrations provide more details that enrich the story. And in some instances, the illustrations and text contradict each other. Marla Frazee's *A Couple of Boys Have the Best Week Ever* takes this delightful contradiction to humorous heights. On one page, the text states that a character arrived "with just a couple of his belongings," while the illustration shows at least five boxes, three bags, and a basket, all overflowing with items. The rest of the book offers more of the same, to hilarious effect.

Aside from the occasional picture book with purposeful contradiction, the text-art interaction should pass scanning for accuracy. Zena Sutherland in *Children and Books* states that children are strictly literal about the pictures agreeing with the words. They understand different styles and techniques, but will not be so understanding if the color stated in the text is not reflected in the illustration, or if the action described in the words appears on a different page in the illustrations.[1]

Some picture books do not consist of intact square or rectangular pages. Lois Ehlert's *Leaf Man* contains pages cut into short spikes or curves on the top, lending a pleasing feel as pages are lifted and turned. *Little Mouse's Big Book of Fears* by Emily Gravett features bite marks, torn edges, and foldouts.

Because many picture book illustrations spread over two pages, how the "gutter" (where the two pages come together in the bound middle) is handled affects the illustration. The artwork should not show uneven matching along this line.

In addition to what is happening inside the book, the size and shape of the physical volume is also important. Whether a book is large, small, square, rectangular, horizontal, or vertical, its physical format was a considered decision made by the designers in relation to the subject of the book.

While picture books rely on the integration of text and art, wordless picture books consist of intriguing illustrations that encourage the young reader to tell the story in his or her words.

Books such as Jerry Pinkney's *The Lion & the Mouse* and Barbara Lehman's *Museum Trip* contain no words. The stories are told entirely through the illustrations. Wordless books offer interesting opportunities for storytelling interaction between the parent, teacher, or other adult reader and the child or children sharing the book.

Whether a parent is reading to a child alone, or a teacher or librarian is reading to a group of children, the adult has purchased or selected the book. Even if the child has picked it out from others on the bookshelf, the adult is usually the reason for that book being on the shelf to be selected. Teachers and librarians in school libraries or media centers read reviews and select books that they think the children will enjoy, but they also consider the curriculum and what books can be used to teach or supplement areas or concepts within it.

By age four, when they would be ready for the titles in this book, most children know the basics of print books: that they have a front and a back, and that a story is inside. Children who have not been read to will need more intensive instruction in the parts of a book in order to ensure literacy and reading success. A good school library or media center program will build upon this with all children to cover more sophisticated concepts concerning books.

The child, then, is ready to hear the story—often many times—and to recognize how it is read. After several readings, the child will be able to, with or without prompting, finish a sentence or chant a repetitive phrase. Asking questions, the adult reader encourages the child to use observation, sequencing, and speculation. The size and energy level of the group dictate the timing of this discussion, either during the story or at the end.

In all cases where picture books are used in instructional activities, adults must not lose sight of the fact that encouraging children to enjoy reading is of prime importance. Reading quality literature because it is an enjoyable leisure activity—that is what children should take away from instruction.

Many resources exist to help integrate picture books into the curriculum of the elementary grades. Some are mentioned in the suggested resources section at the end of this book. Professional publications for teachers and librarians, such as *Book Links,* also carry articles on making picture books an integral part of the curriculum.

While not within the scope of this book, picture books for the older child exist and flourish. Young people do not outgrow picture books even as they move on to chapter books; in fact, some picture books are appropriate only for older readers. Those for the young, including many included here, can be used with older children, especially in art and language arts classes.

TRENDS IN PICTURE BOOKS
Ever-Popular Subjects

Penguins and pirates and pink, oh my! And don't forget the chickens. These subjects abound in recent picture books. Even before the popular documentary *March of the Penguins* (2005), these birds have graced everything from pajamas and plush animals to umbrellas and jewelry. Why not children's books? *Sergio Saves the Game!* by Edel Rodriguez is just one of many, featuring a soccer-loving penguin.

With the popularity of the Pirates of the Caribbean movies and theme park, and the natural attraction to bad-boy behavior, pirates are sailing high. Many of the current books feature comical pirates who take the scary edge off these buccaneers. Books such as Colin McNaughton's *Captain Abdul's Little Treasure* highlight the bumbling pirate.

Type *pink* as a keyword in an online library catalog and see how many picture books show up. Pink is big in clothing, bedspreads, backpacks, barrettes, and anything else marketed to little girls. Whether viewed as just giving them what they want or as a product of the corporate merchandising machine, pink has made its way into picture books. *Pink Me Up* by Charise Mericle Harper stars Violet, who adores the color. Feeling the need to rebel against all things pink? *Not All Princesses Dress in Pink*, by mother-daughter team Jane Yolen and Heidi E.Y. Stemple, acknowledges the longing to be a princess without all of "that color."

Barnyard animals continue their popularity. Cows, chickens, and pigs appear in many books, often anthropomorphized. *Click Clack Moo: Cows that Type* by Doreen Cronin features cows that write letters and protest barn conditions. Pecking, laying eggs, and watching over chicks should be a full-time job for most chickens, but those in some recent picture books have taken to moving out of the henhouse (*Coriander the Contrary Hen* by Dori Chaconas), traveling on a quest (*Buffalo Wings* by Aaron Reynolds), and passing along the latest news (Megan McDonald's *Hen Hears Gossip*). A very realistic pig stars in Howard Mansfield's *Hogwood Steps Out*, where he stays true to his nature. As our society moves further away from its sources of food and many children have no idea what a working farm is like, it is good that barnyard animals remain so prevalent in children's books.

The environment and people making a difference inspire picture book creators. Books about gardening, reflecting its popularity in the adult world, adorn children's shelves. In Peter Brown's *The Curious Garden,* a young boy quietly sparks a revolution in his city with his concern for some plants in his neighborhood. And even garbage, or the disposal of it, makes an appearance in books such as Jonah Winter's *Here Comes the Garbage Barge!*

Picture Books about Art and Books

No doubt reflecting their own passionate feelings about art and books, authors and illustrators have created numerous picture books about these subjects. Appropriately enough, since the picture book represents the marriage of text and illustration, these books encourage the development of aesthetics and an appreciation of art and literature in the young child.

Creativity via artistic expression comes through as the theme in *The Umbrella Queen* by Shirin Yim Bridges. Others books introduce the young child to works of art through plot twists, illustration, or magical enter-the-picture adventure. Mélanie Watt's *Augustine* includes artist-inspired illustrations, which provide a bridge to art appreciation and the recognition of famous works of art. Appendix 1, "Picture Books about Art," lists books that will enhance the development of artistic sensibilities in children. As art education faces budget cuts if not total eradication in some school districts, books about art become more important than ever.

So, too, are the stories that encourage reading and the love of books. In Heather Henson's *That Book Woman,* Cal develops from regarding books as a waste of time to eagerly awaiting the next visit of the Pack Horse Librarian. *Ron's Big Mission* by Rose Blue and Corinne J. Naden ties the passion for reading into a story of a young boy's decision to stand up for his right to check out library books in the 1950s South.

Some books break through the book-reader divide by leaving the story and addressing the reader. By having characters call attention to themselves as characters and to the book as that which contains them, this device creates a postmodern picture book. In *Abe Lincoln Crosses a Creek,* author Deborah Hopkinson speaks directly to the listening audience in several places, figuratively stepping from behind the book to connect with her readers. Illustrator John Hendrix includes illustrations of a hand with a brush and with a pencil, as if the story is being illustrated while read.

In these types of books, a story may be interrupted by a character or narrator giving instructions to the reader, as in *Don't Read this Book!* by Jill Lewis, where even the title gives a clue as to the tone. In others, the entire book consists of a character or characters talking to the reader; in Jef Czekaj's *Cat Secrets,* the wall between reader and story does not exist, with the cat characters looking directly at, and speaking to, the reader.

Mélanie Watt's *Chester* and *Chester's Masterpiece* feature a plot in which the title character has wrested control of the story from the author/illustrator, and their struggle is played out in the pages of these humorous books.

In a classic example, the award-winning *The Three Pigs* by David Wiesner combines dialogue of the characters with surreal illustrations that take the characters out of the ongoing story to form a new story removed from the traditional tale. With pages from the original story that fly across the book into a new setting, this book is a vehicle for a postmodern Three Little Pigs.

Because these books cover a variety of topics and do not easily fit into any particular chapters, an annotated list of some recent titles is presented in appendix 2, "Self-Referential Picture Books."

Cartoon Art

As graphic novels gain in popularity among both adults and teens, their artistic styles and conventions have filtered into picture books. Panels—one of the hallmarks of comics and the graphic novel—are used by the artist to portray actions happening in a sequence. Picture and text integrate tightly in both the graphic novel and the picture book.

Currently, the number of picture books for young children that can be called graphic novels is rather small. A company to watch is TOON Books and Little Lit Library, under the direction of Françoise Mouly and Art Spiegelman (author of *Maus*, the graphic novel for adults), which publishes graphic novels for various age levels, including the very young. Independent publisher Blue Apple Books offers graphic novels in its *Balloon Toons* series. Some mainstream publishers, too, have entered this genre, including Candlewick, which has partnered with TOON Books.

Some artists use elements of the graphic novel in their picture books. In *Otis and Rae and the Grumbling Splunk*, Leo Espinosa uses such graphic novel conventions as word and thought balloons, emotion lines, words as parts of illustrations, and panels. Taking a turn away from the humorous cartoon style, illustrator Patrick O'Brien creates richly expressive worlds on a par with adult graphic novels in Kevin O'Malley's space fantasy *Captain Raptor and the Moon Mystery*.

Whether called cartoons, comic books, or graphic novels, this style influences children's book illustration and bears watching.

EVALUATING PICTURE BOOKS

Text

In evaluating a picture book, one has to consider the text, the illustrations, and the interaction between them. Which is more important: the text or the art? This is not the question; both must work together seamlessly. Because of personal preference, a reader may favor the language over the artwork in a particular book, or vice versa. But critical analysis requires examination of all three factors, whether the objective is to analyze a book for a children's literature course, to evaluate a book for classroom use, or to consider a book for storytime in the library.

Reading the text first silently and then aloud allows one to evaluate the text and to develop a feel for the sound of the book, including language, pacing, rhyme (if it exists), rhythm, and dialogue (if it is part of the story). An important point to consider: will this book hold up to repeated readings aloud? The story must be engaging, appealing to adults as well as children.

Certain subjects will probably always pop up as good material for picture books: a new baby in the house, begging for a pet, school stories, making a friend, the seasons of the year, barnyard animals.

Some books highlight a real person or event, written in a fictional manner, with imagined scenes or characters. For instance, in *The Little Piano Girl,* authors Ann Ingalls and Maryann Macdonald introduce the childhood of composer Mary Lou Williams as a fictionalized story and even give a lyrical swing to the text. Antoine Ó Flatharta's *Hurry and the Monarch,* a look at the life cycle of a butterfly, supplies animal characters with personality and dialogue and, within that fiction, presents biological facts.

Other books feature common experiences, with an author's interpretation. Gillian Shields gives a twist to the standard situation of a child who desperately wants a dog in *Dogfish.* Just as in the title, the story combines two animals by imagining how a little boy's goldfish (his mother's idea of a perfect pet) can act more like a dog. Another common childhood problem, a messy room and toys that spill out into the house, becomes fresh through exaggeration and zaniness in David Shannon's *Too Many Toys.*

Still other books present total fantasy. No child owns a whale in the real world, but a boy does in Mac Barnett's *Billy Twitters and His Blue Whale Problem.* Every page brings a new dilemma as Billy attempts to fit in at school and at play while dragging along the largest animal on earth. In a dreamy vein, *The Weaver* by Thacher Hurd takes place above earth, where the title character weaves the cloth with which she dances over many lands to protect those who are going to sleep.

Like chapter books, novels, and plays, the picture book must hook the reader with its first sentence. It can be funny, incongruous, magical, or mysterious, but it must invite the reader and listener to go on. How the story continues—fast paced, full of action, suspenseful, dreamy—should be appropriate to the plot and theme.

Then it is on to important elements within the story. Evaluate them by asking the questions and considering the aspects of the following areas:

Characters

Who is the main character? Is there more than one? What are the roles of the secondary characters? What informs the characters' actions and makes them unique? How are the characters portrayed? They may be human, animal, or inanimate object. If animal, they may act as humans, as in Nicole Rubel's *Ham and Pickles: First Day of School.* From the text alone, this book could be about human children, but the illustrations feature an animal girl, boy, and classmates. Or the animal characters may act true to their animal nature. In *Grandfather Buffalo,* the animals behave as buffalo would, although author Jim Arnosky allows the reader to experience the old buffalo's point of view.

In Kate McMullan's *I Stink!,* a truck takes on human characteristics, such as speech and thought. Nonmoving objects may also be anthropomorphized, as in Virginia Lee Burton's 1942 classic *The Little House.* In the same vein, the text and illustrations of *The House Takes a Vacation* by Jacqueline Davies portray a house with human characteristics.

Do the characters in the book reflect a worldwide view? Differences in ethnicity, socioeconomic status, age, and gender make for a richer, more realistic story. Some books naturally include these factors as part of the story. Examples include Lenore Look's *Uncle Peter's Amazing Chinese Wedding,* where marriage traditions become an integral part of a personal story; Ellen Levine's *Henry's Freedom Box* and its portrayal of an African American slave who literally sends himself to freedom; and Reeve Lindbergh's *My Little Grandmother Often Forgets* with its three generations of a family. Others portray ethnicity through the artwork, even if it is not intrinsic to the story. *Two of a Kind* by Jacqui Robbins stars African American and Asian girls as the main characters, although this diversity is not the point of the plot. Even a simple illustration of a classroom with African American, Hispanic, Asian, Native American, and other children helps avoid the whitewash that was once the norm in picture books.

In evaluating picture books, look for these diverse types of portrayals. In addition, books in which characters are immigrants or those that feature characters in foreign countries can broaden children's perspectives. Books should either mirror a child's experience (and *all* children should find books about themselves) or widen the child's view. The latter objective takes on even more importance if the child lives in a homogeneous neighborhood and goes to school with children who look like him or her.

Point of View/Tone/Voice

Is the story told from a character's point of view? Or is there an omniscient narrator? What is the mood of the story? What emotions are invoked? Is the story told in first, second, or third person, with first and third being the two most popular?

Setting

What is the time (contemporary, historical, or future)? What is the place (farm, city, apartment, outdoors, foreign country, etc.)? Are they indispensable to the story?

Plot

What happens in the story? What is the problem to be solved or the obstacle to be overcome? What is the outcome? The plot usually is traced as an arc, where the action builds, reaches a high point, and then tapers off to an ending.

Theme

Is there a deeper meaning to the story (for example, friendship, the security of home, love)? This does not mean that the story should be didactic or contain an obvious lesson, but that it reaches beyond simple plot.

Use of Language

Are unfamiliar words used that children will be able to understand within the context of the story? Picture books often use vocabulary above the child's reading level because the books are meant to be read aloud to the child. Even if the child is reading early readers or easy chapter books, the language in the picture book encourages the development of a larger vocabulary. This growth can be enhanced if the parent or teacher calls attention to an unfamiliar word and discusses it with the child.

Is rhyming used? Several categories of picture books incorporate rhyme or the meter of poetry. Some picture books for children consist of a collection of poems, usually about a single theme. For representative titles, see Jack Prelutsky's *There's No Place Like School* or *In the Wild* by David Elliott. Some books that successfully use rhyming text include *Little Black Crow* by Chris Raschka, Alice Schertle's *Little Blue Truck,* and *Come to the Fairies' Ball* by Jane Yolen. For books that do not use rhyming text but incorporate rhythm, pacing, or internal rhyme, see Lauren Stringer's *Winter Is the Warmest Season,* Jonah Winter's *Steel Town,* and Margaret Mahy's *Bubble Trouble.* Look closely at, and read aloud, books that seem to be nonrhyming or straight prose. The best of these use language and rhythm to create text that begs to be read out loud.

Are there elements of repetition? In Michael Ian Black's *A Pig Parade Is a Terrible Idea,* the title line repeats several times throughout the story, after each example of why a pig parade is not good. Doreen Cronin's *Click, Clack, Moo: Cows that Type* features the repetitive sounds of typing and mooing that Farmer Brown hears from his barn, enough times that young readers could be prompted to chime in on the words.

Sometimes the author's words emphasize the repetitive action. Each instance builds the tension until success is met. In David Ezra Stein's *Interrupting Chicken,* the little chicken stops her dad's telling of three fairy tales as she enters each story to inform the characters what to do. The bulk of the book *Nine Animals and the Well* by James Rumford portrays one animal after another showing his or her gift for the raja-king to the animal that came before. The repetition combines a comfortable sense of knowing what comes next with the delicious suspense of wondering what the next animal's gift will be.

Even in stories that do not employ repetition, the sequencing of events provides the dramatic tension in the story, as each event or complication moves the story along from the introduction of the situation on the first page. In evaluating the book, note how this sequencing works as the story progresses.

Illustrations

Evaluating a picture book's artwork begins at the cover. After all, the cover offers a major selling point if displayed with that side up, either in a bookstore or library. The cover illustration may reproduce one of the pages inside, or it may illustrate a unique view of a character or scene; either way, the cover invites the reader in.

In Allen Say's *The Boy in the Garden,* a full-page illustration inside the book appears on the cover cropped, but with the central characters the same size as the inside illustration. Similarly, a cropped picture from inside becomes the back cover illustration.

Illustrated by G. Brian Karas, the front cover of Candace Fleming's *Clever Jack Takes the Cake* features Jack carrying a cake, heading out of the frame of the illustration followed by blackbirds from the story. On the back cover, only Jack's leg is visible as he exits the frame; blackbirds following him lie half out of the frame, too. These pictures do not appear inside the book, although they suggest a major plot point of the story.

The cover art of *The Silk Princess* by Charles Santore provides an example of a wraparound illustration, with the mother and daughter of the story large on the front cover. Other characters and objects trail behind the girl, flowing over the spine and onto the back cover, where strands of silk thread stretch all the way to the edge.

An evaluation of the interior illustrations begins with a silent perusal, as the reader views the artwork with each page turn. Going through the book again without reading the text, but just concentrating on the pictures, allows closer examination.

Color

In many books, the first noticeable visual impact is that of color. The artwork may be multicolored, such as that of Wendy Anderson Halperin in Alice B. McGinty's *Thank You, World* and that of Yuyi Morales in Tony Johnston's *My Abuelita.* Or it may be a limited palette, as in Anushka Ravishankar's *Elephants Never Forget!,* where Christiane Pieper uses black and off-white with blue, and Susan Marie Swanson's *The House in the Night,* in which Beth Krommes illustrates with black and white and gold. Warm colors, such as red, orange, and yellow, or cool colors, in the green-blue-violet range, will evoke different moods and energy.

Blue can mean comfort. Jim Averbeck's *In a Blue Room,* illustrated by Tricia Tusa, stars Alice, who insists that everything around her must be blue before she can fall asleep. The last nine pages of the book, in shades of deep blue after her mother turns off the lamp, signal a change in mood and bring the story to its inevitable end. Green and brown, predominant in illustrations of the natural world, signify life (green, growing things) and even coziness. In *City Dog, Country Frog* by Mo Willems, illustrator Jon J. Muth fills the pages with green in the spring and summer sections, then green and brown and deep orange for fall. During this time, the two main characters share happy moments. When winter comes and frog is gone, the artwork feels cold in its grays and blues. Then spring arrives once more, and the art turns back to greens and happy times again.

In *Oh, Brother!,* a collection of poems by Nikki Grimes, a boy finds himself with an unwanted stepbrother when his mother remarries. Mike Benny's illustration for the poem "Showdown" features a red background, perfect for the confrontational nature of the text and of the artwork: the older boy staring down into the eyes of his stepbrother and pointing his finger at him. Color can also be used as a cultural indicator, as in Kate Aver Avraham's *What Will You Be, Sara Mee?* In several of Anne Sibley O'Brien's illustrations, little Sara is dressed in a traditional Korean *tolbok,* made with rainbow-striped sleeves and a red skirt.

Colors may change from one page to the next when the scene or the mood changes. Robert Ingpen's illustrations of a crowded vessel feature blues, grays, and light violets in Liz Lofthouse's *Ziba Came on a Boat.* As if clearer than her present existence, memories of her life in a war-torn land feature, in many cases, more defined and varied colors. Only toward the end of the book does life on the boat take on brighter hues as Ziba and her mother look to the future.

Line

The many variations of line and shape impact the mood, as well as the characterization and portrayal of action.

In *Sophie Peterman Tells the Truth!* by Sarah Weeks, illustrator Robert Neubecker employs bold black lines to outline the characters and to highlight certain words, indicating the mood of strong negativity toward the little brother. Compare the difference in the delicate lines of *Lost and Found* by Oliver Jeffers, a gentle story of friendship.

The horizontal line separating sky and ground in Grace Lin's *Thanking the Moon* appears in almost every page spread, indicating stability and calm. Contrast this with several scenes in Anu Stohner's *Brave Charlotte and the Wolves,* where Henrike Wilson uses diagonal lines in a forest to represent danger.

Shape

John Segal's *The Lonely Moose* combines geometric shapes with organic. The triangular mountains and pine trees coexist with the irregular shapes of the pond, animals, and deciduous trees, just as the taciturn moose coexists with the bright, bubbly bird. Artists create interesting shapes in the technique of collage with found objects. Hanoch Piven uses everyday school objects as facial features in *My Best Friend Is as Sharp as a Pencil,* such as crayons to represent the art teacher's mustache and an open book that becomes the smiling mouth of the librarian. Observe scale and proportion in evaluating, too. In Matthew Cordell's *Trouble Gum,* almost every illustration is small on each page, even tiny on some, with plenty of white space surrounding. This makes the impact of the final scene huge.

Texture

Does the art look as if it would feel like grass, or a blanket, a rock, or a furry animal hide if it were touched? The texture of the artwork, which depends on the medium and the technique used, adds to the visual style and emotional appeal. Ed Young, in Kimiko Kajikawa's *Tsunami!,* uses various materials in collage illustrations to create fields, water, and houses with touchability. The oil paint of Robert J. Blake's illustrations for *Swift* appears in daubs and lines that give an almost 3-D effect to the landscapes.

Space and Perspective

Whether the artwork appears flat and in the foreground or portrays distant objects in perspective to foreground objects will lend a distinct feel to the story.

A good example of realistic perspective can be seen in Jean Craighead George's *The Last Polar Bear.* In one illustration, illustrator Wendell Minor places a large polar bear so close to the front of the illustration that her whole body does not fit within the pages. Then, to one side of her, a snowy road stretches to the horizon, framed by telephone poles drawn closer together the farther back they go.

Many of the scenes in David Conway's *Lila and the Secret of Rain* feature landscapes that include mountains. Illustrator Jude Daly uses the technique of differing shades to show distance: houses and gardens are dark brown, distant fields are light tan, and the faraway mountains shimmer a bluish white.

Motion

Can a static illustration portray movement? Perry Nodelman in *Words about Pictures* emphatically states that it can, whether in a single image or a series of pictures in which one character is portrayed in different positions or a setting is shown with varying circumstances, implying active movement or transition through time.[2]

Movement across a page spread indicates the forward motion of the story, or the journey of a character from the beginning, through any problems or obstacles, on to the end. Generally, a character moves from left to right across the page spread to indicate this forward movement.

See this in Johannes Hucke's *Pip in the Grand Hotel,* in which Daniel Müller illustrates the children and the mouse chasing, following, and searching from left to right over each two-page spread.

Motion can be shown in illustrations by lines around the character or object suggesting movement, or by the portrayal of the character several times on the page, each time in a different position.

In Denise Fleming's *Buster,* a few page spreads feature four views of the title character in action. Readers and listeners readily understand from the preceding scenes and from the text that there are not four Busters, but that Buster frolicked and ran a long time throughout the day.

Michael Emberley depicts the passage of the school year in Barbara Bottner's *Miss Brooks Loves Books! (And I Don't)*. Several pages of illustrations show school librarian Miss Brooks dressed in costume for various holidays. The accompanying text, with its phrase "all year long," reinforces the fact that all this happens over a span of months.

Composition

Composition—the way the picture is put together with color, line, shape, and texture—offers a myriad of creative possibilities. Bo R. Holmberg's *A Day with Dad* features art by Eva Eriksson in which she composes each illustration with the young boy and his father typically in the middle of the piece. On this day they spend together, they are each other's center. The tightly controlled framing of each illustration, the color pencil texture, and the muted colors with just a splash of red all work together. The composition of *Looking Like Me* by Walter Dean Myers features collages layered with shapes and photographs by illustrator Christopher Myers. Colors that pop, silhouette shapes, and the placement of these elements incorporating the text give a very active sensibility to a book full of energy and pride.

Throughout *Those Shoes* by Maribeth Boelts, illustrator Noah Z. Jones depicts Jeremy as smaller than the other characters. In some of the illustrations, Jeremy wears subdued colors that also symbolize his powerlessness over the situation—wanting the shoes that all the other boys have. But on one page, he is in the center, wearing a red shirt, and large: the page where he finds those shoes, unbelievably, at the thrift store. Later in the story, he is also depicted larger when he makes the decision to give the too-small shoes to another boy.

Media and Technique

Illustrators of artwork in children's picture books work with most media available to artists, including acrylic, oil, watercolor, gouache, tempera, pencil, ink, colored pencil, crayon, chalk, pastel, markers, charcoal, clay, found objects, paper cut or torn (in collage), and wood and linoleum (in printmaking). Artists use a variety of techniques with these media, including painting with brushes or other objects, drawing, printing, collage, photography, or etching. Many of these techniques can be done either hands-on or digitally. Illustrations may also be mixed media, in which the artist uses two or more materials.

TECHNOLOGY

As it has in almost every other field, technology has changed aspects of children's literature. With the advent of the Web in the early 1990s, authors and illustrators embraced this new way of introducing themselves and their work, and publishers took to this outlet for marketing their books. Most authors and illustrators of picture

Artistic Styles

For those who wish to pursue a more detailed analysis of illustrations or learn more about artistic techniques, the suggested resources section at the end of this book contains several good titles, especially those by Shulevitz, Salisbury, and the Withrows. The following styles refer to recognized characteristics in the work of an artist.

Abstract art: The artist uses form and color only as a means of portraying mood in this style. Simple forms and geometric shapes are common. Reality may not enter into what is perceived, although the figures may be recognizable. In his picture book *John Coltrane's Giant Steps,* Chris Raschka employs abstract shapes to depict a box, a snowflake, and raindrops. The kitten that appears is identifiable, but this little animal, too, is all bold black line and shape. An improvisation that is perfect for a book about a jazz classic!

Cartoon art: Nonsensical, preposterous, or exaggerated, these illustrations can run the gamut from mildly amusing to laugh-out-loud funny, from simple to full of details. The popularity of the graphic novel for all ages has brought added prestige for cartoon art. Steven Kellogg, a master of the detailed cartoon, uses this style to great advantage in *The Pied Piper's Magic.* The illustrations containing people, even crowds, feature a great variety of comical facial expressions and poses. Nothing sinister here; even the pictures of rats overrunning the town show a silliness and exaggeration helped along by sunny colors and kaleidoscopic swirls.

Expressionistic art: To communicate the emotion of what is depicted, expressionistic illustrations go beyond reality. Feeling is more important than direct reproduction. Enjoy the carefree, almost wild lines employed by Marjorie Priceman in Kitty Griffin's *The Ride: The Legend of Betsy Dowdy*. There is no doubt as to the emotions on display in each illustration as Betsy goes from worry to determination to fear to exhaustion to relief. The lines and colors mirror this ride.

Folk art: This style arises from the culture portrayed. The art matches the sensibilities and characteristics of a particular ethnic group or nationality. Ben Hodson, the illustrator of Janet Ruth Heller's *How the Moon Regained Her Shape,* uses traditional Native American motifs to illustrate the story and as borders on each page.

Impressionistic art: These illustrations feature a soft undefined line, light, and colors that mix into each other. Not crisp or realistic, the pictures convey just an impression of a scene. In Gloria Whelan's *Yatandou,* the people, buildings, and tools by illustrator Peter Sylvada appear indistinct, although the eye can tell what they are. The texture of the color and the contrast of light and dark enhance the mood of this courageous story.

Naive art: The naive style may look as if the illustrator never learned artistic technique, yet its very simplicity captures the emotion of each scene. Bright and unnatural colors are often used, with no sophisticated perspective aspect. Lynn Rowe Reed employs naive art in *Oliver, the Spaceship, and Me.* Her painted characters exhibit a childlike innocence and sense of fun, with googly eyes, dots for teeth, and curvy hairstyles.

Realistic art: As the name suggests, this artwork represents people, places, and objects as close to reality as possible. For an example, look to Lois Lowry's *Crow Call,* wherein illustrator Bagram Ibatoulline portrays characters and settings of the 1940s. His people look lifelike in face and body. Details such as wisps of hair, curved fingers, the set of a mouth, and the bend of a knee are ultrarealistic. How appropriate for the story of a girl and her father reconnecting after he has been to war.

books maintain personal websites as a way to reach out to their audience. In some cases, a website for an individual title may be created. Teachers and librarians can find some great information for author studies and classroom activities on the sites. Cynthia Leitich Smith's website (www.cynthialeitichsmith.com), well organized and easy to use, includes teacher guides for her books as well as information, interviews, and "blogbuzz." Packed with resources, Jan Brett's site (www.janbrett.com) features activities, including bulletin boards and "how to draw" videos. In addition to entering individual's names in a search engine to find their sites, lists of author and illustrator websites with links can be found on compiled websites, such as one page in the American Library Association's Great Websites for Kids (gws.ala.org).

In order to connect personally with their readers and publicize their work, picture book authors and illustrators may use social networking tools such as Facebook and Twitter. Some maintain blogs or post YouTube videos. These outlets, unimagined a few years ago, provide information for librarians, teachers, and others keeping up with favorite authors and artists on their existing works and upcoming titles.

Taking technology to a core audience for picture books, some websites provide digital children's books. One of the best known is the International Children's Digital Library (http://en.childrenslibrary.org), with more than 4,000 books from around the world in fifty-five languages. Children's librarians seeking picture books in a child's native language, teachers investigating multicultural themes, or parents looking for additional sources of books can view these full text volumes; the site also makes available apps to download the books to an iPhone or an iPad.

Digital Illustration

An area where technology has changed the very making of the picture book is illustration. An artist can now create a picture book illustration entirely on a computer.

More common is the process in which the artist draws by hand, digitally scans that drawing, then uses software to select and add color, change the size, add layers, create texture, and complete the illustration digitally. This software enables illustrators to create art that looks as if it were produced using their favorite media or technique, painted with a specific kind of brush, for example, or on a certain type of textured paper. Some artists draw with a pen and graphics tablet, which preserves the hands-on artistic technique but takes advantage of the technology by producing the drawing on a computer rather than a piece of paper. Collage illustrations can be created using Photoshop. Found objects, photographs, and items from nature can be manipulated and layered with the other elements of the composition.

Working digitally allows the illustrator to edit, change, and try out ideas without permanently committing them to paper. The copyright page of the book often states what media were used in the illustrations of a picture book. Check there to see if digital techniques were part of the process.

E-Books and Apps

Where do picture books fit into a world bursting with e-books? Dedicated devices for adult books and children's books without illustrations are great for their purpose, but when Apple introduced the iPad, followed by Barnes & Noble's NookColor, picture books as e-books became possible. These devices allow the view of a page spread instead of one page at a time, absolutely necessary for picture books. They also make possible the ability to display in color, another must.

An adult can read picture books on e-readers or tablets to a child, or can activate the option to have it read by a narrator. The books can be read on an e-reader, tablet, or smartphone. For large groups, the librarian or teacher can connect the iPad to a projector. Words that pop up as they are read, animation in the illustrations, entertaining music, the ability to bookmark a page—all these make the e-book fun and can enhance literacy instruction.

E-books are generally available in a format such as EPUB or PDF, two of the most popular. Apps refer to the applications, or software, that are downloaded. An app to read e-books may be downloaded to an e-reader. Or apps that are e-books can be downloaded; these books are more interactive, allowing children to do more with the story, such as tapping or clicking on objects within scenes. Additional activities, including coloring and games, or features such as changing to a different language, may also be part of the package.

More than two-thirds of public libraries now make e-books accessible to their patrons, and just over a quarter offer access to e-book readers.[3]

For libraries considering the purchase of e-readers, price is of course a concern, but so is possible obsolescence of the device in a few years. E-reader technology is changing rapidly. As for e-books themselves, availability of titles is an issue. Will every new picture book also be available as an e-book? Licensing is still being hammered out, as are digital rights management (DRM) issues such as who owns electronic rights and questions of access, including number of checkouts allowed, whether simultaneous checkouts are permitted, and interlibrary loan.

New developments in e-books, e-readers, and apps are emerging. Look for new products and applications in the months and years ahead.

USING THIS BOOK

Mirroring the child's social development, this book begins with the child's personal concerns and family relationships and then moves out into the community and on into the larger world. A chapter on imaginative books is included, followed by one containing folktales and fairy tales. Each chapter gathers a variety of outstanding books with wonderful stories and beautiful illustrations.

So open this book to read about some of the best in recent children's picture books. Then open a picture book with a child and enter the world where words and art come together.

Notes

1. Zena Sutherland, *Children and Books* (New York: Longman, 1997), 119.
2. Perry Nodelman, *Words About Pictures* (Athens: University of Georgia, 1988), 159.
3. Judy Hoffman, John Carlo Bertot, Denise M. Davis, and Larra Clark, *Libraries Connect Communities: Public Library Funding & Technology Access Study 2010–2011*. Digital supplement of *American Libraries*, June 2011. Available at http://viewer.zmags.com/publication/857ea9fd. 7, 24.

······ 2 ······

My Family and Myself

The picture books in this section represent the child's comfort zone. Primary relationships with parents, grandparents, or siblings make up the stories. The books feature everyday concerns, such as going to sleep, wanting a pet, welcoming a new baby, or visiting Grandma and Grandpa's house. The characters are human, or can be animals if anthropomorphized. Some of the stories are set in other countries or cultures but concern universal feelings and experiences.

....

Ashman, Linda   **4–8 YEARS**
WHEN I WAS KING
Illustrated by David McPhail
New York: HarperCollins, 2008 | 978-0-06-029051-1

A look at the experience of being a big brother, this story is told from the point of view of the dethroned "king." He reveled in his role as the center of attention, but now his parents and grandparents dote on his baby brother. The baby even plays with his toys. But when the baby chews on his baseball glove and big brother has a meltdown, his mom gives him sympathy and reminds him of how much he can do that little brother cannot. With rich colors and facial expressions that reveal a range of emotions, the illustrations complement the text and its moods of resentment and anger, then pride and love. The font shows what is important: certain words are larger, especially *I* and *mine*. Any older child who has had to deal with sibling rivalry will relate to the king. For a big sister-little sister variant, see *Rosie and Buttercup* by Chieri Uegaki (Kids Can, 2008).

Averbeck, Jim
IN A BLUE ROOM
Illustrated by Tricia Tusa
Orlando: Harcourt, 2008 | 978-0-15-205992-7

Anyone who has ever resisted going to sleep, or who has dealt with a child doing the same, will relate to this book. While her mother entices Alice with flowers and tea and a quilt, the little girl insists that each item be blue. Finally, when her mother turns off the lamp, the moonlight turns everything in her room that color, and she can finally sleep. The ink, watercolor, and gouache illustrations reflect Alice's restlessness, but then, as the blueness of the moonlight comes in, create a mood of peace and rest. The text and illustrations capture perfectly the illogic of Alice's demands and the magic of the color-changing properties of moonlight. Pair this with Jonathan Bean's *At Night* (Farrar Straus Giroux, 2007), the story of a little girl with insomnia who finally finds rest on a rooftop, and Mij Kelly's *William and the Night Train* (Farrar Straus Giroux, 2000), where a wide-awake boy finds sleep on the train to Tomorrow.

Avraham, Kate Aver
WHAT WILL YOU BE, SARA MEE?
Illustrated by Anne Sibley O'Brien
Watertown, MA: Charlesbridge, 2010 | 978-1-58089-210-0

In first person, big brother Chong explains the Korean celebration of *tol*, for a baby's first birthday, to his baby sister and to the readers. He looks forward especially to *tolja-bee*, a game where the birthday child selects from a number of objects; what she picks is an indication of her future. Ink-and-watercolor illustrations show Chong and Sara, their parents, grandparents, and other relatives and friends in a celebratory mood, enhanced by bright colors and some traditional costumes. Bold black lines surround the colors and provide a pleasing contrast. Throughout the story, the family speculates on little Sara's future occupation by what she seems to enjoy. A glossary of Korean words and an author's note at the end offer more information about this celebration.

Banks, Kate
MAX'S WORDS
Illustrated by Boris Kulikov
New York: Frances Foster/Farrar Straus Giroux, 2006 | 978-0-374-39949-8

A little brother, outshone by his stamp-collecting and coin-collecting older siblings, discovers something that interests him. Max now collects words by cutting them out of publications and eventually makes them into sentences and then stories. The marvelously quirky illustrations feature differing points of view, dependent upon scene:

a bird's-eye view of the older brothers' collections, Max in a chair with the words displayed in front of and larger than him, and a small Max and his brothers entering into a story of a worm and a large crocodile. The words Max collects progress from simple typescript to colorful and shapely; the word *pancakes* features round and tan letters, *hissed* portrays two green snakes as the *ss*'s. Continue witnessing the power of words with *Max's Dragon* (Farrar Straus Giroux, 2008), where Max and his brothers search for rhyming words.

Billingsley, Franny   **4–8 YEARS**
BIG BAD BUNNY
Illustrated by G. Brian Karas
New York: Richard Jackson/Atheneum, 2008 | 978-1-4169-0601-8

This book provides a splendid example of the use of contrast in story and illustration. Entering this story from the title page, readers and listeners may believe that it is about a mean rabbit threatening a small animal's house in a tree stump. But through the course of the narrative and enhanced by the illustrations in gouache and acrylic with pencil, the rabbit is not who he appears to be. The illustrations of the Big Bad Bunny appear wild and drawn in an almost childlike way (note the mean black eyebrows). His splashing and gnawing and stomping come alive through the action and color of the drawings. In contrast, the illustrations of the house where Mama Mouse takes care of her babies exude calm and orderliness. Although green is the dominant color, because much of the action happens outside, bright splashes of orange and red bring out the fierceness of the title character. At its heart, this is a story of a mother's love for her child who has imagined an alter ego and then become frightened by it.

Bradford, Wade   **5–9 YEARS**
WHY DO I HAVE TO MAKE MY BED? OR, A HISTORY OF MESSY ROOMS
Illustrated by Johanna van der Sterre
Berkeley, CA: Tricycle/Random House, 2011 | 978-1-58246-327-8

The old adage "The more things change, the more they stay the same" rings true as the theme of this book. A little boy does not want to make his bed because he feels he has already done too many chores. His mother tells him about his grandmother, who said the same thing in 1953, when she heard the story from her mother about her grandfather, who said the same thing in 1911, and back through history. The playful illustrations, in watercolor and digitally finished, depict the rooms, beds, and toys of the children; the year is also part of the illustration. The repetition of the title question is amusing, while the enumeration of particular chores is instructive. A good book for discussion (notice how the number of toys decreases as history rolls back), this would also work as a supplement to social studies. At the end of the book, a two-page "Chores through the Ages" provides information on children's lives and playthings from prehistoric times through the present day.

Brown, Peter   4–8 YEARS
CHILDREN MAKE TERRIBLE PETS
Illustrated by Peter Brown
New York: Little, Brown, 2010 | 978-0-316-01548-6

In a twist on the familiar child-wants-a-pet plot, this story features a little girl bear who wants a child. As soon as Lucy sees the "critter" in her part of the forest, she knows that he is the perfect pet for her. True to form, Mother Bear says all the things that a human mother would say. The illustrations, a combination of pencil, construction paper, wood, and some digital, feature an appealing Lucy and her adorable little boy enjoying typical activities together. The text of the narrative is set off in rectangular boxes, while dialogue appears in word balloons of a different color, hand-lettered by Brown. Illustrations are bordered on each page with a thin frame of different-colored woods, corresponding to the forest setting. All good things must end, as Lucy discovers when her pet boy goes missing, but a twist on the last page provides a humorous ending and speculation for what comes next in her search for a pet. With the almost universal theme of wanting a pet, the cross-species behaviors, and humorous situations, this book will appeal to most readers and listeners. For a read-alike, see *C'mere, Boy!* by Sharon Jennings (Kids Can, 2010).

Bruchac, Joseph   3–7 YEARS
MY FATHER IS TALLER THAN A TREE
Illustrated by Wendy Anderson Halperin
New York: Dial/Penguin, 2010 | 978-0-8037-3173-8

Thirteen different pairs of dads and sons fill the pages of this celebration of a father's love and support. Each two-page spread contains a large illustration across the top, with four smaller illustrations in a band below, and then text in a narrow band at the bottom. The beautifully textured art features a diverse group of fathers who differ ethnically and in other ways. There is a father who looks like a grandfather. One of the fathers is blind, with a guide dog and cane. In each setting, the father and son enjoy activities that any child could relate to: walking in the park, playing hide-and-seek, making faces. For those children who call their father something other than Dad, the names Pop, *mi papá*, Pa, and Papa appear. The very last page turn reveals twenty-four small squares, each with the fathers and sons from throughout the book participating in even more fun activities. A beautiful look at the father-son bond, through all seasons, in many parts of the country, and with many loving fathers.

. . . .

Cole, Henry   3–8 YEARS
TRUDY
Illustrated by Henry Cole
New York: Greenwillow/HarperCollins, 2009 | 978-0-06-154268-8

Esme is one lucky little girl. Her farmer grandfather tells her that they will find a pet for her at the auction. After searching, they finally find one they can both agree on: Trudy the goat. Esme loves her new pet. Soon family, friends, and neighbors realize that Trudy is special, too, for she can forecast when it will snow. But as winter deepens, Trudy gives up her weather-predicting ways in order to concentrate on something even more special. This gentle book portrays the love of grandparents and granddaughter, as well as the love of a little girl for her farm pet. Read-alouds will be fun as the dialogue lends itself to the interpretation of grandfather's gruff, yet gentle sentiments and neighbors' enthusiastic comments. The illustrations, rendered in acrylic paints, seamlessly combine pastoral quietness and the activity of chores with a bit of humor. The browns and tans of autumn give way to the whites and blues of winter as time passes and readers head for the payoff: Trudy and her baby, who seems to have a forecasting ability of her own.

. . . .

Cordell, Matthew   4–8 YEARS
TROUBLE GUM
Illustrated by Matthew Cordell
New York: Feiwel and Friends, 2009 | 978-0-312-38774-7

The cover gives a mighty big clue to the story this book holds: a small pig has blown a huge pink bubble that encircles the words of the title. Then there are the front endpapers, full of big and small bubbles being blown by the same pig. In the story, the bubble-blowing pig, Ruben, receives some gum from his visiting grandmother. While his mother recites the gum rules to Ruben and his little brother, Julius (you can just tell they've heard these before!), Ruben gets busy chewing his in all sorts of positions and motions. All this is hilariously pictured in small black, gray, red, and pink drawings. Action words portraying the unwrapping, snapping, stretching, and smacking accompany, and become part of, the illustrations. Readers can anticipate the trouble of the title as Ruben systematically ignores his mother's three rules and finally makes a giant bubble mess in the largest picture of the story. Be sure to notice the final endpapers, similar to the front ones, but full of popped bobbles. Ruben takes naughtiness to the most entertaining level.

Crow, Kristyn   **5–9 YEARS**
THE MIDDLE-CHILD BLUES
Illustrated by David Catrow
New York: G. P. Putnam's Sons/Penguin, 2009 | 978-0-399-24735-4

Oh, to be the middle child, between an older brother and a baby sister who can seemingly do no wrong and who get all the privileges. With a text that imparts the rhythm and the pacing of a blues song, and the pencil-and-watercolor illustrations that wackily portray people and events, the story introduces the forgotten child. The humor carries through with garish colors that culminate at an amusement park, where middle child Lee sings his song and plays his guitar to hordes of other middles, including his parents. Check his pompadour and shirt collar, which go into full Elvis mode by the end of the story. A marvelous example of illustrations that add an extra layer to the text, in this case with goofiness and the put-upon demeanor of Lee. Contrast to Elizabeth Winthrop's *Squashed in the Middle* (Holt, 2005), which has a more realistic and gentle tone.

Crowe, Carole   **4–8 YEARS**
TURTLE GIRL
Illustrated by Jim Postier
Honesdale, PA: Boyds Mills, 2008 | 978-1-59078-262-0

Magdalena waits for the annual arrival of the sea turtles with her grandmother. As the turtles lay their eggs in the sand, the girl protects them from predators and garbage on the beach. When her grandmother dies, a heartbroken Magdalena becomes angry. But sadness and hope mingle in the story, as eventually she goes out to the beach to witness the newly hatched turtles making their journey back to the sea. The realistic illustrations reflect the wonder of this part of the turtles' journey, the wisdom being passed from one generation to the next, and Magdalena's sadness at her grandmother's passing. (See figure 2.1.) Rich blue-and-green illustrations match the sea, but also the characters' clothing, providing continuity. Skillfully rendered, the illustrations of the turtles are awe inspiring.

Crum, Shutta   **4–8 YEARS**
THUNDER-BOOMER!
Illustrated by Carol Thompson
Boston: Clarion/Houghton Mifflin Harcourt, 2009 | 978-0-618-61865-1

Crum and Thompson take readers and listeners through a summer storm in the country. A farm family, consisting of parents and two children, feel a change in the weather, see the darkening sky, and run for shelter just before the rain and hail hit.

Figure 2.1   *Turtle Girl*

Humorous illustrations, in watercolor, gouache, pastel, crayon, and collage, capture the excitement and fear of a potentially damaging storm. The side story of Maizey the hen and her strange behavior is resolved when everyone discovers she was protecting a kitten. The text, with strong verbs, is just right for a storm story. The author's poetry background shows in her phrases that arouse the senses. Readers will almost be able to feel the humid air of a languid summer day, hear the frenzy of wind and rain and hail, and finally smell the after-rain. Sounds and bits of dialogue become part of the illustrations, which make it all seem very immediate. A good story to supplement a discussion about storms or farms. A complement to this, *Like a Hundred Drums* by Annette Griessman (Houghton Mifflin, 2006), also portrays a thunderstorm in a rural area.

Denise, Anika   3–8 YEARS
BELLA AND STELLA COME HOME
Illustrated by Christopher Denise
New York: Philomel/Penguin, 2010 | 978-0-399-24243-4

A wonderful example of illustrations completing a story, this book takes on a common childhood experience—moving to a new house. Reading the text only, one would assume that two children leave the old house, ride to the new house, explore rooms, unpack, and spend a first night there. But the illustrations, pencil and digital, tell a different story: a little girl and her stuffed elephant experience these events. In some of the illustrations, especially where emotions run high, Stella the elephant is portrayed as huge. In others, she appears as a normal-sized toy. The ending introduces the neighbors, including a little boy with a stuffed giraffe. Obviously, these two will be friends, as the last page shows them playing cards with imaginary giant-sized animals. This story comforts as it tackles a standard childhood situation with gentle humor and a steadfast friend.

Falconer, Ian   4–8 YEARS
OLIVIA FORMS A BAND
Illustrated by Ian Falconer
New York: Anne Schwartz/Atheneum, 2006 | 978-1-4169-2454-8

Many "diva" books have appeared recently, but Falconer's Olivia titles belong near the top of the heap. With rather spare illustrations—notice the effective use of shading to add depth and texture—the books feature an anthropomorphized young pig who clearly sees herself as the center of attention of her family. The facial expressions and reactions of her parents and two younger brothers reinforce the humor that emanates from Olivia and her wild ideas. In this title, she becomes a one-woman band to accompany fireworks. Parents and teachers will recognize familiar situations and conversations; young readers and listeners will identify with the irrepressible and ever-creative Olivia. Everyone will respond to the humor, both broad and sly, as they enter into Olivia's world. Colorful illustrations in charcoal and gouache consist of black, white, and gray, with splashes of red and blue; several pages, especially in the fireworks scenes, contain much more color on a dark background. Look for Olivia's "Supreme dream" on the final page, which gives an idea of her ego.

Gravett, Emily   4–8 YEARS
LITTLE MOUSE'S BIG BOOK OF FEARS
Illustrated by Emily Gravett
New York: Simon & Schuster, 2008 | 978-1-4169-5930-4

A collection of fears could be scary, but this book makes them manageable. Little Mouse acknowledges her fears on each page spread, conveniently labeled with the particular phobia portrayed. A stunning array of these fears, some common (fear of spiders) and some not (fear of clocks), come to scary life through the illustrations of Little Mouse and her pencil. A color scheme of muted shades of tan, with black and white and occasional splashes of red and blue, lends an air of secrecy and fear. The illustrations, oil-based pencil and watercolor, also contain found objects. Several pages feature foldouts: of a newspaper, a map, and a postcard. Pages with chewed corners and illustrations of spills continue the theme of a little mouse creating the book as the reader pages through. Never fear! The twist ending makes it all worthwhile.

Grimes, Nikki   **5–10 YEARS**

OH, BROTHER!

Illustrated by Mike Benny
New York: Amistad/Greenwillow/HarperCollins, 2008 | 978-0-688-17294-7

When his *mami* remarries, Xavier gains a stepfather plus a stepbrother, Chris. In a series of twenty short poems, Xavier tells the reader all about his resentment and his battles with Chris. But along the way, he finds out why Chris feels he has to be the perfect child and what happened to his mother. Each poem is a perfect jewel of a feeling, an event, or an emotion that Xavier works through. The gouache illustrations reflect these feelings, some realistically and some symbolically. For example, on one two-page spread, Xavier on a pizza in outer space looks on as his mother and the two interlopers play on another pizza on the facing page. In another, a tiny Xavier cowers on a page filled with the huge feet of his stepdad and stepbrother. A wonderful book for the study and appreciation of poetry, for the portrayal of a blended family that many students will relate to, for the depiction of an interracial family (Hispanic and African American), and for a story with a truly happy ending.

Harper, Charise Mericle   **4–8 YEARS**

PINK ME UP

Illustrated by Charise Mericle Harper
New York: Alfred A. Knopf/Random House, 2010 | 978-0-375-85607-5

Violet, a little bunny who is gaga over the color pink, is disappointed when her mother is too sick to go to the Pink Girls Pink-nic. But that's putting it mildly; with her exuberant body language and excitable language, Violet leaves no one guessing what she thinks. The character that gets to "pink up" is none other than her daddy. Bright cartoon illustrations—heavy on pink, of course—feature Violet and members of her family and friends with hilarity. The text features many exclamation points and differing font sizes and is integrated around the illustrations. This book is geared to those who cannot get enough of the color pink, but it also offers a spirited story about a dad who is a good sport. Contrast the tone with Nan Gregory's *Pink* (Groundwood, 2007), which delves into class differences and envy.

Harrington, Janice N. **4–8 YEARS**
THE CHICKEN-CHASING QUEEN OF LAMAR COUNTY
Illustrated by Shelley Jackson
New York: Melanie Kroupa/Farrar Straus Giroux, 2007 | 978-0-374-31251-0

Told in first person by a little girl who loves to chase chickens, this story delights in action, attitude, and surprise. Her prime target is Miss Hen, plump and beautiful—and a good runner. The lively collage illustrations present each chicken as an individual. Notice the fence as music staff and other collage elements in the clothes and food. Cutout letters, which make up the title in the cover art, pop up throughout the book to represent the squawks of the birds. Lest adults think that the chicken chaser can indulge only in an activity that is forbidden by her grandmother, she does eventually become a responsible caregiver to chickens and chicks.

Heo, Yumi **4–8 YEARS**
TEN DAYS AND NINE NIGHTS
Illustrated by Yumi Heo
New York: Schwartz & Wade/Random House, 2009 | 978-0-375-84718-9

The title provides a clue to the story, which establishes a countdown from the time a little girl and her father see her mother off on a flight to Korea. There the mother will complete the adoption process, and the little girl will have a baby sister. The illustrations portray both the mother in Korea and the little girl preparing her home with the help of her father and grandparents. A calendar shows the countdown, as well as the text, which provides the written number of days and nights left. Colorful illustrations in oil, pencil, and collage show happy faces and a lot of busy activities on both sides of the ocean. An author's note about Korean adoptions concludes the book. For a story about a baby girl adopted from India, with the father flying over, see Uma Krishnaswami's *Bringing Asha Home* (Lee & Low, 2006). *My Mei Mei* by Ed Young (Philomel, 2006) portrays the adoption of a baby from China.

Holmberg, Bo R.   **4–8 YEARS**

A DAY WITH DAD
Illustrated by Eva Eriksson
Cambridge, MA: Candlewick, 2008 | 978-0-7636-3221-2

A young boy of divorced parents makes the transfer between his mom and his dad at the train station. When his father arrives, they immediately plan their day. As they go from a hot dog stand to a movie to a pizza place to the library, the mood is happy. A wonderful portrayal of the love between father and son, this story evinces no sense of abandonment but acknowledges that time together is short. The illustrations, in colored pencil, always show the father and son as the center of attention in each drawing. (See figure 2.2.) Colors are muted, as if in a memory being savored, although Dad's red scarf stands out in many of the drawings. A comforting, reassuring story for children who do not live with their father.

Figure 2.2   *A Day with Dad*

Jenkins, Emily   **4–8 YEARS**
THAT NEW ANIMAL
Illustrated by Pierre Pratt
New York: Frances Foster/Farrar Straus Giroux, 2005 | 978-0-374-37443-3

A couple of dogs are not happy that a new baby has joined their human family. Missing the special attention they once received from the grown-ups, one of them contemplates what they could do to the new little one, but the other one wisely deters her. Eventually they become protective of the baby, not letting Grandpa, whom they have never met, near him. Full of gentle humor, the text shows from a dog's point of view what it is like to deal with an intruder. The colorful illustrations emphasize the baby as the center of attention, with the parents always surrounding and leaning over him. At the end, the two dogs and baby are on the couch, obviously at home with each other, but then turn the page and see that Mom is pregnant again, and readers can speculate about who will be unhappy next.

Johnston, Tony   **4–8 YEARS**
MY ABUELITA
Illustrated by Yuyi Morales
Boston: Houghton Mifflin Harcourt, 2009 | 978-0-15-216330-3

Full of love for his grandma, a young boy describes her and her activities around the house. With colorful illustrations made from a variety of materials, including clay, fabric, wood, and metals, the book is a visual delight. Throughout the narrative, Spanish words pop up as Abuelita cooks breakfast, dresses, and prepares for work. Although her work is alluded to throughout the story, not until the last page do readers find out what it is. So many positive emotions and attitudes combine here: love between a grandmother and grandson, pride in one's appearance, keeping in shape for one's work, and enthusiasm for life. From little Frida Kahlo the cat to Abuelita's fuzzy robe to her bumblebee towel, there is much to smile at in this story.

Joosse, Barbara M.   **3–8 YEARS**
GRANDMA CALLS ME BEAUTIFUL
Illustrated by Barbara Lavallee
San Francisco: Chronicle, 2008 | 978-0-8118-5815-1

The love of a grandmother for her grandchild fills this book with an atmosphere of tenderness and care. Set in Hawai'i, with some Hawaiian words and traditions employed, the story features a grandmother who tells her granddaughter how beautiful the child is and has been from the day she was born. Watercolor illustrations, bright with the color of sun-drenched islands, focus on the two main characters, although other villagers, animals, and vegetation appear. Their gentle lyricism matches and expands the text, which features poetic elements and back-and-forth dialogue. End material includes a glossary of Hawaiian words and a string design that children can make, similar to a cat's cradle. Complement with Denise Vega's *Grandmother, Have the Angels Come?* (Little, Brown, 2009), which also contains alternating dialogue and charming illustrations, but which focuses on the grandmother's appearance.

Juster, Norton   **3–7 YEARS**
THE HELLO, GOODBYE WINDOW
Illustrated by Chris Raschka
Michael Di Capua/Hyperion, 2005 | 978-0-7868-0914-1

The love and security of the grandparents' home comes through in this story of a child visiting their house, and what happens at the kitchen window. As the child describes the kitchen and what Nanna and Poppy do there—play the harmonica, count the stars, make breakfast—the everyday activities create an atmosphere of love. The energetic and colorful illustrations appear childlike in their simplicity yet project a masterful combination of color, line, space, and mood. A special story about a special window, which represents the fun and feeling shared by a child and her grandparents, this book was the Caldecott Medal winner in 2006. Nanna, Poppy, and their granddaughter return in *Sourpuss and Sweetie Pie* (Michael Di Capua/Scholastic, 2008).

Khan, Rukhsana   **4–8 YEARS**
BIG RED LOLLIPOP
Illustrated by Sophie Blackall
New York: Viking/Penguin, 2010 | 978-0-670-06287-4

When her mother insists that Rubina take her little sister along to a birthday party of one of her classmates, Rubina just knows that this is not the way it is done in their new country. She feels embarrassed and, as she fears, little Sana makes a scene. Even worse, Sana steals her red lollipop, a treat which she has been saving from the party. The text, in first person, allows the reader or listener to feel Rubina's conflicting emotions of excitement and chagrin. Some illustrations put the characters at center stage, with (on most pages) very little or no background. Several illustrations show movement with lines of motion or direction; one, in which Rubina runs from her school to home, shows the blocks and sidewalks behind her, and another, where Rubina chases Sana through the house, looks down from the top at the pieces of furniture and rugs. When time passes and Sana receives a party invitation, her mother insists that she take the youngest sister, Maryam. Rubina remembers her experience and talks to her mother, a satisfying ending to a very realistic story about sibling rivalry.

Lammle, Leslie   **4–8 YEARS**
ONCE UPON A SATURDAY
Illustrated by Leslie Lammle
New York: HarperCollins, 2009 | 978-0-06-125190-0

How does an author get inside the head of a character, especially one with a great imagination? Lammle's portrayal of young June is pitch-perfect. Before she can do all the fun things she dreams up, June must finish a list of chores. With a little help from a bird, a dragon, and under-bed monsters, she finishes her tasks. Illustrations in watercolor and pencil portray June and her fantasies in comical fashion. In some cases, the creatures become as large as she is. This and the list that towers over her head contribute to the feeling of being overwhelmed by her chores. Dialogue balloons pop up in several scenes as June addresses her imaginings and her mother brings her back to reality. This adventurous girl (check out the goggles and flashlight) is a character to amuse and inspire.

Lewin, Betsy   **3–7 YEARS**
WHERE IS TIPPY TOES?
Illustrated by Betsy Lewin
New York: Atheneum/Simon & Schuster, 2010 | 978-1-4169-3808-8

With rhyming and minimal text on each page, this story follows a cat and his daytime activities. His nighttime activities, however, remain a mystery until the last page. Young listeners will enjoy the cutouts on certain pages: a mouse hole, two circles to see the cat's eyes, and diecut pages that become a moon and a blanket, among other items. The artwork illustrating Tippy's daytime perambulations features bright colors in sunny yellow, orange, and green. The nighttime scenes shimmer with a pale yellow moon and textured blue sky that spills over into blue fence posts and blue blankets. A fun bedtime story for family read-alouds, this book would also be useful for teachers planning lessons on time or night and day.

Lindbergh, Reeve   **4–8 YEARS**
MY LITTLE GRANDMOTHER OFTEN FORGETS
Illustrated by Kathryn Brown
Cambridge, MA: Candlewick, 2007 | 978-0-7636-1989-3

This story of a grandparent with memory loss, handled gently and respectfully, focuses on her relationship with her grandson. The rhyming text recounts incidents of her misplacing objects, losing her way, and calling the grandson by his dad's name, but it also describes how the grandson helps her. The illustrations, in watercolor and ink, display a delicateness and detail in a mixture of indoor and outdoor scenes. Far from being sad, this story told from the point of view of the young boy is rather matter-of-fact. For another take on this subject, but still with grandson-grandmother characters, see *A Young Man's Dance* (Boyds Mills, 2006) by Laurie Lazzaro Knowlton. For a granddaughter's point of view, see Robin Cruise's *Little Mamá Forgets* (Farrar Straus Giroux, 2006) and the Belgian import *Still My Grandma* by Véronique Van den Abeele (Eerdmans, 2007).

Look, Lenore   **4–8 YEARS**
UNCLE PETER'S AMAZING CHINESE WEDDING
Illustrated by Yumi Heo
New York: Atheneum, 2006 | 978-689-84458-4

A wedding in the family should bring great joy, but one little girl is not happy. In first person, she takes the reader through the whole day and expresses her displeasure at what she feels is her uncle's abandonment of her. Along the way, she explains many Chinese wedding traditions. Her words, which express her emotions and describe the customs as a young girl would, are enhanced by the oil paint, pencil, and collage illustrations. The cartoon-style artwork fills up each page with all the objects she describes and all the people at the wedding, including a large extended family. Despite her attitude, the story does not turn negative but instead reveals both her openness to express herself and the many traditions she explains. At the end, Uncle Peter's new wife finds a way to connect with his niece, and it all ends on a happy note.

Lowry, Lois   **5–9 YEARS**
CROW CALL
Illustrated by Bagram Ibatoulline
New York: Scholastic, 2009 | 978-0-545-03035-9

With beautiful language, Lowry tells a story based on her girlhood in which she ventures out with her father, newly returned from the war. Tentatively, she reconnects with him, eventually confiding her fears and reveling in a shared sense of humor. Realistic illustrations of watercolor and acryl-gouache complement the narrative visually with emotion and period detail. Although set in the 1940s, this story will resonate with any listener who shares, or wishes to share, quality time with Dad. The outdoor setting will appeal to many, and the notion of calling the crows with a whistle may be new to almost everyone. Read this lovely father-daughter story and revel in the superb use of language by a master storyteller.

Myers, Walter Dean
LOOKING LIKE ME
5–10 YEARS

Illustrated by Christopher Myers
New York: Egmont, 2009 | 978-1-60684-001-6

With energy and poetry, with vibrant color and exuberant line, this book celebrates being proud of one's self, one's place in the family, and one's place in the world. The father-and-son team who wrote and illustrated this book have given a gift to all young people who read it, especially boys. Jeremy, the main character, receives affirmation from his sister, father, teacher, grandmother, friends, and mother amid a swirl of saturated color, silhouettes, and photographs. The rap-like rhythm of the words encourages reading out loud; at the same time the words call for thoughtful contemplation. The collage illustrations invite exploration. (See figure 2.3.) This would be an excellent source to use in art classes of all ages. The book ends with a page about the author and illustrator that contains small pictures of the young Walter and Christopher surrounded by words describing them.

Pitzer, Susanna
NOT AFRAID OF DOGS
4–8 YEARS

Illustrated by Larry Day
New York: Walker, 2006 | 978-0-8027-8067-6

Daniel has a problem. His family must take care of his aunt's dog, but Daniel is afraid of dogs, even though he will not admit it. Although he tries to hide from Bandit, he forms a bond with the pet when he discovers they are both afraid of thunderstorms. The illustrations, in pen and ink with watercolor and gouache, capture Daniel's fear of dogs, his stubbornness, and his eventual realization that the dog is more fearful than he is. The realistic text gets Daniel's dialogue just right, as he insists that he is not afraid, he just does not like dogs. At the end, of course, he completely reverses his opinion, and even lets Bandit sleep in his bed. A book of comfort to those children who may be afraid of dogs, and a feel-good book about man's—or boy's—best friend.

Ransom, Jeanie Franz
WHAT DO PARENTS DO?
(WHEN YOU'RE NOT HOME)
4–8 YEARS

Illustrated by Cyd Moore
Atlanta: Peachtree, 2007 | 978-1-56145-409-9

A young boy imagines what his parents are up to while he and his little sister visit their grandparents. Everything he envisions, hilariously illustrated in watercolor and colored pencil, is something that he obviously has been told not to do, such as jumping on the bed with shoes on, sitting too close to the television, and playing basketball in

HE PUT OUT HIS FIST.

I GAVE IT A BAM!

I'M JEREMY, BROTHER, AND MY FATHER'S SON.

Figure 2.3   *Looking Like Me*

the house. The text even contains his words of disapproval, which sound exactly like something parents would say. While Mom and Dad inhabit the main illustration on each page, small scenes of the boy and his sister at the grandparents' house provide a counterbalance, as they do the right thing and still have fun. Parents who share this book with children will chuckle in recognition, and children will appreciate the misbehaving antics of the grown-ups.

Ritz, Karen   **4–8 YEARS**
WINDOWS WITH BIRDS
Illustrated by Karen Ritz
Honesdale, PA: Boyds Mills, 2010 | 978-1-59078-656-7

A young boy moves from a house to an apartment, but this story is told from the point of view of his pet cat. In first person, the cat remembers what was, and how it is now so different. No back story is provided to explain why the move has occurred, but certain words that appear in the text (misery, quiet, tossing and turning) and the boy's somber look in one of the early illustrations make it seem that it was not a happy one. But, as often happens, a new day brings a fresh perspective. The cat discovers that birds still fly outside the window, that this new place also has lovely hiding places, and that his boy still comes home to him. Realistic watercolor artwork features large illustrations of the cat, the boy, and other objects in the home, making readers or listeners feel as if they are there.

Rosen, Michael J.   **4–8 YEARS**

A DRIVE IN THE COUNTRY
Illustrated by Marc Burckhardt
Cambridge, MA: Candlewick, 2007 | 978-0-7636-2140-7

The twisting roads around country sites that fill the endpapers provide a preview to what readers will find inside this story of a stock family experience: the Sunday drive. A family—Mom, Dad, three kids, and a dog—take a trip with no real endpoint. They stop at various places along the way, driving down curving roads in a beautiful countryside portrayed in acrylic illustrations. A combination of full two-page pictures, bordered one-page illustrations, and smaller scenes in circles provide variety. Told in first person, the text reads as if a friend is telling about all the fun things he did. The rich colors of the illustrations, the leisurely pacing of the story, and the solid feeling of family combine in this congenial story.

Rosenthal, Amy Krouse   **4–8 YEARS**

ONE OF THOSE DAYS
Illustrated by Rebecca Doughty
New York: G. P. Putnam's Sons, 2006 | 978-0-399-24365-3

Everyone has had one of those days, and this book names them specifically. With this clever concept, each page, or sometimes a two-page spread, presents the type of day in word and picture. Favorite Pants Too Short Day, Itchy Sweater Day, Can't Find Stuff Day—see them all here. The illustrations, in paint and ink, show a young boy or girl undergoing the trial of that particular day. Comical drawings and bright colors make the artwork kid friendly. While some of the days are laugh-out-loud humorous, others are poignant. This book would be a great discussion starter on feelings and bouncing back from disappointments. *One of Those Days* is one of those books that enters into a child's sensibilities and understands.

Rylant, Cynthia   **4–8 YEARS**
ALL IN A DAY
Illustrated by Nikki McClure
New York: Abrams, 2009 | 978-0-8109-8321-2

How can the concept of time be explained to a child? This seemingly impossible task might be just a bit easier if this book is used to describe "a day." With rhyming text, Rylant makes clear how a day's newness signifies hope and that anything can happen. McClure's illustrations depict a young boy in a country setting, with chickens and a garden, with dandelions and a hammock, with walks in the woods and a sudden rainstorm. (See figure 2.4.) An artist's note at the end explains the process of making the cut-paper illustrations, including how the colors—alternating gold and pale blue with each page turn—were added by computer. The overall scheme of black and white with just one color combined with the unique illustrations is beautifully spare on some pages and remarkably detailed on others. Altogether, it evokes moods of happiness and satisfaction, which work well with the poetic text. In the last scene, the little boy walks toward the rising sun, shovel over his shoulder, ready to meet the new day as the text encourages listeners to seize the day and make it their own.

Sanders-Wells, Linda   **4–8 YEARS**
MAGGIE'S MONKEYS
Illustrated by Abby Carter
Somerville, MA: Candlewick, 2009 | 978-0-7636-3326-4

What is real, and are there situations where it just does not matter? A big brother figures this out when his little sister tells the family that pink monkeys now live in the refrigerator. Everyone else in the family—Dad, Mom, and older sister—go along with Maggie's notion. But her brother keeps reminding everyone that the monkeys are not real. Told in first person from his point of view, the story builds on his frustration with his family and their acceptance of these monkeys. But one day, when his friends visit and start teasing Maggie, he comes to her defense and stands up to his friends. With every question they ask, he counters with the answers that other members of his family have given him. Illustrations, in black colored pencil and gouache, portray the family in cartoon style with bright colors. The brother's frustration and the other family members' benign acceptance come through clearly and humorously in the artwork. An impish twist: some of the illustrations feature a pink border; some of these include a little pink monkey crawling along the side or perched on top. This is a lively story about family loyalty and the magic of imagination.

Figure 2.4 *All in a Day*

Shannon, David   **4–8 YEARS**

TOO MANY TOYS

Illustrated by David Shannon
New York: Blue Sky/Scholastic, 2008 | 978-0-439-49029-0

Shannon's signature humorous situations and giddily goofy illustrations make this book a delightful experience for children and adults. When Spencer's mother finally reaches her limit with the mess in his room, she insists that he get rid of some of his toys. And who can argue with her? Just about every page bursts with toys of all kinds. Glorious color and realistic text detail what types of toys Spencer plays with and where the toys came from. Two scenes of special note: Spencer giving his mother the big-eyed, aw-mom look when she dares to try to throw out a dirty old stuffed bunny, and Spencer in an office setting as he argues his case to negotiate a deal with his mother for keeping the toy train. Genius! Adults will laugh with recognition, and kids will relate to Spencer in this slice-of-life adventure.

Shea, Bob   **5–9 YEARS**

BIG PLANS

Illustrated by Lane Smith
New York: Hyperion, 2008 | 978-1-4231-1100-9

Considering its big size (9.5 by 13 inches), its huge type fonts, and its over-the-top braggadocio, this book has the perfect title. A look inside the head of a boy who has been placed in the corner of his classroom, the story features his imaginings: from taking over a business meeting, to winning a football game, all the way up to being the president and then an astronaut. The mixed-media and collage illustrations complement perfectly the wacky, no-holds-barred nature of the story. Anyone who secretly has dreamed of being the boss of everyone will enjoy this book.

Sheth, Kashmira   **4–8 YEARS**

MONSOON AFTERNOON

Illustrated by Yoshiko Jaeggi
Atlanta: Peachtree, 2008 | 978-1-56145-455-6

A young boy in India finds a willing playmate in his *dadaji*—his grandfather—on a rainy afternoon. They race boats, watch a peacock, visit the banyan tree so the little boy can swing and pick mangoes. This sweet tale transcends nationalities as it portrays the love between a grandson and grandfather and the simple joys of playing and observing nature. (See figure 2.5.) The two also talk about what the grandfather did as a young boy and imagine what the present little boy will do when he is a grandfather.

Figure 2.5 *Monsoon Afternoon*

When his grandmother scolds them for tracking in mud, the boy and his grandfather even take on the same sheepish expression. The watercolor illustrations, soft and muted, reflect the rainy day. Their view of an Indian street, courtyard, and house will be interesting for children who are just learning about cultural differences.

Shields, Gillian   3–7 YEARS
DOGFISH
Illustrated by Dan Taylor
New York: Atheneum/Simon & Schuster, 2008 | 978-1-4169-7127-6

What can a boy do when his mother insists that he does not need a dog and that his goldfish is just as good a pet? The first-person narrative lends immediacy to his story; he also throws in comments on the feelings the characters portray—sad, irritated, hopeless—which are then reflected in the illustrations. Overall, a mood of humor comes through as son and mother trade reasons for and against, and as the boy tries to treat his goldfish like a dog. The illustrations, rendered digitally, are spare and modern looking. The round heads of the characters match the round goldfish bowl, round goldfish, and round head of the imaginary pet. A delightful charmer of a story over a familiar battle. Supplement with Emma Dodd's *What Pet to Get?* (Scholastic, 2008), where a little boy comes up with all kinds of wild ideas that his mother shoots down; *You?* by Vladimir Radunsky (Harcourt, 2009), where a girl finds a pet in the park; and Fiona Roberton's *Wanted: The Perfect Pet* (Putnam's, 2009), in which a duck convinces a boy that he is ideal.

Stein, David Ezra   **4–8 YEARS**
INTERRUPTING CHICKEN
Illustrated by David Ezra Stein
Somerville, MA: Candlewick, 2010 | 978-0-7636-4168-9

Just as the title promises, this story features a chicken who insists on interrupting the bedtime stories that her papa tells. One after the other, favorite tales such as Hansel and Gretel, Little Red Riding Hood, and Chicken Little do not make it past the second page, as the chicken bursts in with words of warning to the storybook characters. The illustrations—in watercolor, crayon, china marker, pen, opaque white ink, and tea—abound in reds, greens, and blues and feature the characters with exaggerated heads and tail feathers. The pages that open up to the storybooks depict an immediate change; not only the fact that an open book is pictured, but the illustrations change to muted colors and a limited palette. So when the little chicken literally enters the story, her bright colors contrast. The repetition of the three stories with three interruptions leads to the little chicken writing and illustrating her own story, done in childlike drawings and letters. A sweet ending finally brings rest in this story of a familiar bedtime ritual. Another animal that likes to interrupt stories, this time a dog, stars in Peter Catalanotto's *Ivan the Terrier* (Atheneum/Simon & Schuster, 2007).

Stevenson, Robert Louis   **4–8 YEARS**
THE MOON
Illustrated by Tracey Campbell Pearson
New York: Farrar Straus Giroux, 2006 | 978-0-374-35046-8

A poem by the famous nineteenth-century author Stevenson forms the text of this picture book. The watercolor-and-ink illustrations depict a young boy going out for a nighttime boat ride with his father. At first glance, the story told in the pictures has little to do with the poem, but each line contains elements reflected in the illustrations. A mood of adventure and fun permeates the trip out to the boat, the boat ride, and the trip back home. The moon appears on every two-page spread, except for the very last, when morning has come. Sharp eyes will notice that in that scene the little boy runs to his parents with the book *The Moon*. An excellent example of illustrations complementing text, with neither explaining the other, this book could be used as a learning opportunity for poetry. This might even be one that children will memorize on their own with enough repeat readings.

Sullivan, Sarah   **4–8 YEARS**
ONCE UPON A BABY BROTHER
Illustrated by Tricia Tusa
New York: Farrar Straus Giroux, 2010 | 978-0-374-34635-5

More than just another pesky little brother story, this book combines the bothersome brother with the creativity of the writing process. Lizzie loves to make up stories, and when her little brother, Marvin, comes along, he becomes part of her plots. Although he is a pain, he unwittingly helps her overcome her writer's block. Everyday scenes of school and home life take on a charming cast with humorous illustrations and stories within the story. Little extras like Lizzie's special Princess Merriweather pencil and Marvin's many messes add to the giggles. The text makes clear the writing process, including its highs and lows, and brings home the point that stories are best when shared.

Swanson, Susan Marie   **3–7 YEARS**
THE HOUSE IN THE NIGHT
Illustrated by Beth Krommes
Boston: Houghton Mifflin, 2008 | 978-0-618-86244-3

A comforting reverie about home combines with fantasy, as a girl flies on the back of a bird over her town and up above the moon. The rhythm of the text makes it a delight as a read-aloud. A wonderful example of precision of language, the text combines seamlessly with the detailed illustrations. With three colors—black, white, and gold—Krommes provides the reader with the whole world from a single room to outer space. Each of the double-page spreads contains one or more objects of the bright color, highlighted in the scratchboard illustrations. This book was a Caldecott Medal winner in 2009. Readers may feel its kinship to Margaret Wise Brown's *Goodnight Moon,* as well as the cumulative story of The House That Jack Built.

Viorst, Judith   **4–8 YEARS**
JUST IN CASE
Illustrated by Diana Cain Bluthenthal
New York: Ginee Seo/Atheneum, 2006 | 978-0-689-87164-1

Charlie, who always imagines the worst, believes in being prepared. Viorst's text humorously details his imagined fears and his sometimes over-the-top preparations, such as digging a pit in his yard for a lion that may get loose. The illustrations in mixed media match the gentle humor in his imagined scenarios and his complicated preparations. In the end, a surprise birthday party truly takes him by surprise—it is one situation for which he has not prepared. The sometimes crazy things Charlie does will appeal to children, who will identify with his worry and with his imagination. The illustrations, presented simply with lots of white space, feature bright colors and incorporate collage. A good choice for read-alouds or for one-on-one sharing.

Wardlaw, Lee   **4–8 YEARS**
WON TON: A CAT TALE TOLD IN HAIKU
Illustrated by Eugene Yelchin
New York: Henry Holt, 2011 | 978-0-8050-8995-0

Telling a story within a demanding form is difficult; Wardlaw makes it look effortless as she uses senryu, a form of Japanese poetry. Like haiku, senryu is a poem of three lines, with five syllables in the first, seven in the second, and five in the third. Clearly expressed, Won Ton's journey from an animal shelter to a new home shows humor, attitude, and growing affection for his new family. Illustrations rendered in graphite and gouache on watercolor paper offer spare visuals—usually just Won Ton and an object or two on each page—which coordinate beautifully with the text. The endpapers feature a great expanse of cat fur that matches Won Ton's grayish blue fur throughout the book. Besides being a heartwarming story of a rescue animal, this book is an excellent supplemental source for the study of haiku and senryu for any age group.

Weeks, Sarah   **4–8 YEARS**
SOPHIE PETERMAN TELLS THE TRUTH!
Illustrated by Robert Neubecker
New York: Beach Lane, 2009 | 978-1-4169-8686-7

The truth that Sophie feels compelled to tell concerns babies. This humorous look at being a big sister is told in the first person, accompanied by illustrations that go beyond the words in expressing how perfectly awful her little brother is. The text includes lots of large, hand-drawn words and phrases that convey Sophie's disgust and exasperation. The cartoon-style illustrations, in India ink and colored digitally, come on strong, just like the title character. An articulate big sister, Sophie reveals her irritation but eventually finds that she does like the little guy. This book will appeal to all kids who think their younger siblings are monsters. Pair with *How to Be a Baby—by Me, the Big Sister* (Schwartz & Wade, 2007) by Sally Lloyd-Jones. See this plot turned upside down in James Solheim's *Born Yesterday: The Diary of a Young Journalist* (Philomel, 2010), in which a baby explains her sister.

Wong, Janet S.   **4–8 YEARS**
HOMEGROWN HOUSE
Illustrated by E. B. Lewis
New York: Margaret K. McElderry/Simon & Schuster, 2009 | 978-0-689-84718-9

No place is quite as comforting as a grandmother's house, as the girl in this story discovers when she is faced with moving to yet another new place. She recalls her family's previous three houses and wonders at her parents' need to move again. Enveloped in the love of Grandmom, she relates the things that they like to do together revolving around the grandmother's house and its importance to her. The lovely watercolor illustrations pick up this theme with scenes of the girl and her grandmother gardening and cooking. Grandmom's comments reveal her to be feisty, a positive thinker, and loving toward her grandchild. This story and the impressionistic illustrations wrap the reader in a blanket of a grandparent's love.

Woodson, Jacqueline   **4–8 YEARS**
PECAN PIE BABY
Illustrated by Sophie Blackall
New York: G.P. Putnam's Sons/Penguin, 2010 | 978-0-399-23987-8

Sibling rivalry before the new baby actually arrives is not uncommon. In this story Gia resents the coming baby whom everyone, it seems, cannot stop talking about. Even her friends' jump rope rhymes are about babies. Notice Gia's size in some of the illustrations where she is feeling especially crowded out by talk of, and preparation for, the new baby. Ink-and-watercolor illustrations depict an African American girl and her mother, with multiethnic school friends and relatives. This story sweetly captures the mixed emotions of a big sister who feels her relationship with her mother will be changed forever.

Yolen, Jane, and Heidi E. Y. Stemple   **3–8 YEARS**
NOT ALL PRINCESSES DRESS IN PINK
Illustrated by Anne-Sophie Lanquetin
New York: Simon & Schuster, 2010 | 978-1-4169-8018-6

For all those girls going through the princess phase, this book reinforces the idea that girls can play sports, get dirty, fix things, and enjoy many fun activities. They may still wear their princess crowns, but they also dress in sports jerseys, jeans, overalls, and bike helmets. The delightful digital illustrations feature a diverse collection of active girls, all with their crowns. Teachers, librarians, and parents may want to use this story, a nice antidote to the plethora of pink, to let both girls and boys know that many facets to one's personality and many different interests can coexist. The rhyming text comprises between two and four lines per two-page spread, which keeps the story rolling along to the final scene, a royal ball with all manner of clothes—but no pink! Pair with Mary Hoffman's *Princess Grace* (Dial, 2008), in which Grace and her classmates learn about real princesses throughout history and the world, shattering several stereotypes.

······ 3 ······

In My Community

I n the picture books in this section, the main relationships portrayed exist outside the family, but still within the community. The books represent a moving out to other places, with a potential for fear, but also great fun. The realization that every family is not like one's own family, a necessary step in maturity, may be explored in discussion. Separate sections for friends and school are included.

Addy, Sharon Hart   **4–8 YEARS**
LUCKY JAKE
Illustrated by Wade Zahares
Boston: Houghton Mifflin, 2007 | 978-0-618-47286-4

Jake and his pa, panning for gold in the West, find one nugget. This takes them to a store where Jake finds a pet pig, which inadvertently guides them to their real treasure: establishing a restaurant and shop. Events leading to consequences that build upon one another carry the story along, as the father and son become planters, cooks, and traders of goods. Although Pa always invokes luck, it is hard work and clever trading that bring them success. The large illustrations, rendered in pastels, capture the spirit of life during the Gold Rush. Rich-hued colors of deep purple, orange, and green establish a mood of warmth. The love between father and son, though never overtly expressed, is evident, as are Jake's feelings for his pig, the real initiator of luck. Though not romanticizing the Old West, *Lucky Jake* makes it relatable to today's children.

Ashman, Linda 4–8 YEARS
CREAKY OLD HOUSE: A TOPSY-TURVY TALE OF A REAL FIXER-UPPER
Illustrated by Michael Chesworth
New York: Sterling, 2009 | 978-1-4027-4461-7

With a pleasantly rhyming text and comically busy illustrations, this story tells the tale of a large family in a dilapidated house and what happens when the doorknob falls off. Various members of the family come up with ideas to fix it, with outside help, which build in a daffy succession until the family finally decides they must design an entirely new home. First-person voice lends an insider feel to the goings-on. Note the placement of the ink, watercolor, and pencil illustrations on each page, and the use of white space to surround them and to hold the text. Some illustrations feature cutaway views of the house, allowing readers to see the location of each family member. Others offer a bird's-eye view, looking down at a large scene of activity. And every page is busy; with eight people in a multigenerational family, plus a dog, an atmosphere of fun and cooperation bursts through. The illustrations reflect the words of the text and add more detail. In the end, the baby resolves the doorknob problem, simply and sweetly, and the family decides they love their house as is.

Blue, Rose, and Corinne J. Naden 4–8 YEARS
RON'S BIG MISSION
Illustrated by Don Tate
New York: Dutton/Penguin, 2009 | 978-0-525-47849-2

Ron's mission on the day of this story is to become the first African American to obtain a library card and check out books at Lake City Public Library in South Carolina in 1959. The kindly head librarian knows him as the boy who loves to read and even considers him her best customer, although he has been allowed to read the books only at the library. On this day, he asks to check out books and even stands on the counter in order to make his case. After the police and his mother are called, the head librarian decides to issue him a card. The text brings out Ron's determination and sense of purpose. Illustrations in rich colors feature Ron in the center of most scenes. Airplanes in the sky in several pictures foreshadow his future. In addition to celebrating the love of reading, this fictionalized story will introduce young listeners to a time of segregation and to a young boy who stood up for his rights. An author's note at the end tells the rest of Ron McNair's story: he grew up to become an astronaut, one of the crew of the space shuttle *Challenger* in 1986.

Bridges, Shirin Yim
4–8 YEARS

THE UMBRELLA QUEEN
Illustrated by Taeeun Yoo
New York: Greenwillow/HarperCollins, 2008 | 978-0-06-075040-4

The struggle of an artist between producing for money and creating from the heart shines through this story, set in Thailand. Noot eagerly joins the women in the village business of painting umbrellas. While she can paint competently the flowers and butterflies that have long been the local tradition, she really loves to paint elephants. Although her family expresses displeasure with her choice of subject, she is vindicated when the king comes through the village to inspect the umbrellas and names Noot Umbrella Queen for the New Year holiday. The illustrations, linoleum prints with pencil, feature fine lines in the scenes of both industrious work and busy village life. These complement and expand the text, which also relates how umbrellas are made and how the villagers interact. Shades of orange, gold, and turquoise predominate, with pink and blue elephants making a delightful contrast. Take note of the endpapers: the front with traditionally painted floral umbrellas, the back with elephants on the umbrellas.

Brown, Tameka Fryer
4–8 YEARS

AROUND OUR WAY ON NEIGHBORS' DAY
Illustrated by Charlotte Riley-Webb
New York: Abrams, 2010 | 978-0-8109-8971-9

Acrylic illustrations full of expressive energy and movement, coupled with poetic text, will make readers want to live in this neighborhood. A young girl makes various stops at local spots—for ice cream, at her uncle's barbershop, past chess-playing neighbors—in order to get home in time for the block party. Bringing in the foods, music, and activities of the party, the author and illustrator together celebrate a community of various ethnicities and ages. Notice the great rhythm of the text and the unconventional rhyming.

Croza, Laurel
4–9 YEARS

I KNOW HERE
Illustrated by Matt James
Toronto: Groundwood/House of Anansi, 2010 | 978-0-88899-923-8

Although a number of children's books treat the situation of moving to a new home, this story concerns a little girl and her family who are part of a small group temporarily living in trailers while working on a dam-building project in Saskatchewan. The families find that they will next move to Toronto, and therein lies the tension in the story. In expressive language that evokes the senses, the girl enumerates what she knows—the road where she lives, the forest where she plays, the creek where her sister catches frogs. When her teacher has the children draw pictures of their memories of this place to take to Toronto, the girl draws many of the things she has known and seen. Richly colored illustrations enhance her feelings of excitement tinged with nostalgia. Several of them frame the text in interesting ways—for example, on the pull-down map in the classroom, in a drawing of an eye, and on that piece of paper she folds up with her memories. The endpapers offer an artist-drawn map of Canada, from the province of Saskatchewan to the city of Toronto, with animals and plants native to Canada adding visual detail. The small size of the book makes it personal, too. An evocative look, told in first person, at the lives of workers who must follow the job.

Cunnane, Kelly   4–8 YEARS
FOR YOU ARE A KENYAN CHILD
Illustrated by Ana Juan
New York: Anne Schwartz/Atheneum, 2006 | 978-0-689-86194-9

Following the lead of the title, the text is presented in second person, addressed to a young boy as he proceeds through one day. He herds cows, visits villagers, plays with his friends, and even gets into trouble. Acrylic-and-crayon art portrays the villagers and animals expressively, especially their eyes. In addition to mirroring the action of the text, the illustrations also provide details of a Kenyan village. The text includes several Swahili words; a glossary at the beginning of the book provides definitions and pronunciations. Listeners will relate to the child who, like children everywhere, forgets to do his chores in the face of other, more interesting activities.

Daly, Niki   4–8 YEARS
RUBY SINGS THE BLUES
Illustrated by Niki Daly
New York: Bloomsbury, 2005 | 978-1-59990-029-2 | paper

A little girl's booming voice torments the people in her neighborhood and at school until she takes singing lessons and learns to channel her sound. Cartoon-style illustrations, rendered in pencil and ballpoint pen and digitally enhanced, make Ruby's story appealing. Musical motifs on her voice teacher's dress and her school concert costume, as well as the designs on her painter-mother's dress, add an artistic flair. Her loudness is illustrated with hand-lettered words, very large in the pictures. Touches of humor appear, such as her teacher attempting to teach Ruby to use her shirt buttons as on, off, and volume control. Endpapers exude a jazzy style, with bright colors and line drawings of musical instruments and symbols.

Henson, Heather
4–8 YEARS

THAT BOOK WOMAN
Illustrated by David Small
New York: Atheneum, 2008 | 978-1-4169-0812-8

A boy who has no use for reading or books, and who looks down on his sister who loves them, finds a slow-growing admiration for a woman on horseback who brings free books to his mountain home. A beautiful tribute to the Pack Horse Librarians who delivered books in the Appalachians during the Great Depression, this book shows great respect for an illiterate boy as it tells the story from his point of view. Illustrations, rendered in ink, watercolor, and pastel chalk, use pale colors to show the isolation and hardscrabble life of the mountain people. The text employs Appalachian dialect and believably shows the transition from suspicion to appreciation to a desire to read that occurs in Cal. And what facial expressions he is given! They, too, show this change throughout the course of the story. The book concludes with an author's note on the Pack Horse Librarians and a list of websites and books about them. For another fictionalized story based upon a real librarian, read Gloria Houston's *Miss Dorothy and Her Bookmobile* (HarperCollins, 2011).

Ingalls, Ann, and Maryann Macdonald
4–8 YEARS

THE LITTLE PIANO GIRL
Illustrated by Giselle Potter
Boston: Houghton Mifflin Harcourt, 2010 | 978-0-618-95974-7 | library binding

This fictionalized version of the early life of Mary Lou Williams introduces young readers and listeners to this important jazz pianist and composer. The rhythm and words of the text fit the musical theme, enhanced by charming illustrations of Mary Lou, her family, and neighbors. Even the layout of the text in some areas recalls a musical scale, as each line is indented in from the one before. By concentrating on her childhood, the story should appeal to children who can relate to Mary Lou's move to a new town, encounters with bullies, and embarrassment over her shoes. The gouache illustrations feature many scenes of Mary Lou playing the piano, which was her passion and her talent from an incredibly young age.

Johnson, Dinah
4–9 YEARS

HAIR DANCE!
Illustrated by Kelly Johnson
New York: Henry Holt, 2007 | 978-0-8050-6523-7

Braids, puffs, dreadlocks, straightened: this book is a celebration of the hairstyles of African American girls. In a variety of color photographs, these girls embody beauty and pride, joy, and reflection. The pacing and the diversity of styles and moods are designed to appeal to young girls. The author's note about culture and the photographer's introduction about her grandparents' beauty salon add context and background. A list of further reading for kids and grown-ups appears on the last page. A wonderful example of photographic illustration, this book also features poetic text set on colorful stripes and blocks of a rainbow of colors.

Lin, Grace   3–7 YEARS
THANKING THE MOON: CELEBRATING THE MID-AUTUMN MOON FESTIVAL
Illustrated by Grace Lin
New York: Alfred A. Knopf, 2010 | 978-0-375-86101-7

A nice introduction to the Chinese Moon Festival, this story follows a family—Ma-Ma, Ba-Ba, and three daughters—out into the country for a picnic and party. With special foods and lanterns, the family becomes part of a large group on the hillside, picnic blankets spread with treats and lanterns lit to mimic the moon. Gouache illustrations, colorful yet reflecting a dark blue nighttime sky, show the mooncakes, smiling steamed cakes, pomelos, and Asian pears, as well as the equipment needed for the lanterns. Autumn leaves in some illustrations remind readers that this is a harvest festival, celebrated in the fall. The endpapers feature simple illustrations of the objects used in the family's picnic, which readers and listeners can then look for within the pages of the story. A two-page author's note at the end explains the Mid-Autumn Festival and how Asian families celebrate this holiday.

Martin, Jacqueline Briggs   5–8 YEARS
THE WATER GIFT AND THE PIG OF THE PIG
Illustrated by Linda S. Wingerter
Boston: Houghton Mifflin, 2003 | 978-0-618-07436-5

Gorgeous acrylic illustrations and moving text combine wonderfully in this story about a grandfather told from his granddaughter's point of view. Like the stories of his days as a sea captain, the style is one of long ago. Grandfather seems to have lost his gift for finding water with a divining rod. When his pet pig—the last offspring of the pig he kept onboard his ship—goes missing, he gives up completely. With the help of his granddaughter, he locates the pig and witnesses the return of his gift for finding water. The illustrations, beautifully textured, convey broad swaths of sea, fields, and roads contrasting with detailed faces. A mixture of warm and cool colors accentuates the tugging of the sea and the land for both grandfather and the little girl. Readers and listeners may want to investigate further the phenomenon of divining rods and finding water with a forked stick.

McGhee, Alison   **6–9 YEARS**
SONG OF MIDDLE C
Illustrated by Scott Menchin
Somerville, MA: Candlewick, 2009 | 978-0-7636-3013-3

A perky little piano student practices constantly in order to prepare for a recital. Simple yet appealing illustrations, done in pen and ink and colored digitally, will appeal to those following the story of her preparation and then her problem when she forgets what she has memorized. Told in first person, the story reveals the girl's formula for success: imagination, lots of practice, and lucky underwear. Who knows which one helps as she overcomes her trial of forgetfulness? Students who have experienced recitals of any kind and those who like to read or listen to stories about plucky heroines will enjoy this one.

Newman, Lesléa   **4–8 YEARS**
MISS TUTU'S STAR
Illustrated by Carey Armstrong-Ellis
New York: Abrams, 2010 | 978-0-8109-8396-0

In this book, ballet is for everyone, no matter what size or shape. Selena loves to dance even though she is not the most graceful when she begins her lessons. Comical illustrations in gouache and colored pencil present Selena as energetic and full of mistakes but willing to work to improve. Look for the facing pages that show the progress of the class from one year to the next. Pages where Selena appears large and at the center of attention intersperse with pages where she is just one of many in the ballet class, or where she feels small and scared before the recital. A feeling of joy flows throughout the story, even through dancing difficulties, and culminates at the recital. Notice the long scarf in the audience that binds together Selena's family and friends; sharp-eyed readers will see her mom knitting this scarf in earlier illustrations. One of the best things about this book is its depiction of the heroine as not ultrathin or especially coordinated. She is real. She is brave. She follows her passion.

Pelley, Kathleen T.   **4–8 YEARS**
RAJ THE BOOKSTORE TIGER
Illustrated by Paige Keiser
Watertown, MA: Charlesbridge, 2011 | 978-1-58089-230-8

So many positives in this story: its depiction of an independent bookstore, pride in oneself, and handling a bully. A cat believes himself to be a tiger because his owner, a bookstore owner, tells him so and the customers at the store treat him that way. When an interloper cat joins him in the store and sets him straight, it takes the poetry of

William Blake and a guest author to restore his pride. Watercolor-and-colored-pencil illustrations feature fine lines and varied colors that capture Raj's moods and the activity in the bookstore, as well as the affection that everyone has for the bookstore tiger.

Robert, Na'ima B.   **4–8 YEARS**

RAMADAN MOON
Illustrated by Shirin Adl
London: Frances Lincoln, 2009 | 978-1-84507-922-2

A young girl explains the Muslim month of Ramadan, with its activities of fasting, prayer, and charity. In the prose poem text, she relates how her immediate family spends the month, but she also connects it to Muslims in her community and around the world. Illustrations of watercolor, collage, and color pencils feature fine lines, a multitude of colors, and interesting textures. Notice the backgrounds on each page and the variety of materials used: crushed tissue paper to portray the sky and water, a collage of postage stamps, paper printed with Arabic symbols, and more. Fabrics, photographs, and detailed drawings provide visual appeal. The first and last pages frame the story and reflect the title, with references to the moon. Lyrical language and child-friendly art make this book an effective introduction to this Islamic religious observance for the young. Pair this with Maha Addasi's *The White Nights of Ramadan* (Boyds Mills, 2008).

Schwartz, Joanne   **4–8 YEARS**

OUR CORNER GROCERY STORE
Illustrated by Laura Beingessner
Toronto: Tundra, 2009 | 978-0-88776-868-2

A young girl helps out in her grandparents' grocery store, a small mom-and-pop business that provides fresh produce, breads, sandwiches, and candy to neighborhood customers. Anna Maria goes through the day, explaining what she does in the store to help her Nonna Rosa and Nonno Domenico. Sweet illustrations—colorful in the array of products for sale, the store environment, and the neighborhood—make the store one that anyone would want to visit. For those who live in a small town or neighborhood where such stores still exist, the story may seem familiar. For adults for whom this type of store resides only in the past, this will be a trip down memory lane that they can share with students and children.

Smith, Cynthia Leitich   4–8 YEARS
HOLLER LOUDLY
Illustrated by Barry Gott
New York: Dutton/Penguin, 2010 | 978-0-525-42256-3

The title becomes the name of the main character, a boy who just cannot speak quietly. From the time of his birth, Holler is LOUD. A succession of humorous scenes illustrates his loudness and its effects on a classroom, at the movie theater, and out fishing with his grandfather. Even the text of his words appears much bigger—and in color—than the rest of the text on the page. The entire town finally tells him to hush, but then a big storm approaches and his volume saves everyone. The cartoon drawings perfectly match the humorous, over-the-top mood of the text, with plenty of details in the diverse crowd scenes to provide new sights in each reading. Look for the surprise twist at the end, as the town discovers a way to honor Holler's loudness.

Spalding, Andrea, and Alfred Scow   6–9 YEARS
SECRET OF THE DANCE
Illustrated by Darlene Gait
Victoria, BC: Orca, 2006 | 978-1-55143-396-7

When the Indian agent tells the elders of a Canadian tribe that their dancing is forbidden, they travel to a remote village for a potlatch ceremony. There a young boy watches the dance that portrays the stories of his people. The illustrations combine black and white with color to reflect the mood of each scene. For example, at the potlatch, the colors of the masks and costumes show as boldly colorful reds and greens. In addition, almost every illustration includes paintings of tribal symbols or animals that the young boy sees as he looks out the window or pulls aside a curtain. Based upon author Scow's childhood witnessing of the dance, this story provides a wonderful opportunity for discussions about discrimination and traditions of First Nations. The cover illustration features a young boy's eyes; the back cover, an old man's eyes. Includes a historical note and glossary.

Underwood, Deborah   3–7 YEARS
THE QUIET BOOK
Illustrated by Renata Liwska
Boston: Houghton Mifflin, 2010 | 978-0-547-21567-9

Hush! Celebrating the many types of quiet in a child's life, this book projects a gentle mood. Small animals acting as children star on each page, as the text presents the kind of quiet illustrated. Solitary activities such as coloring appear, as do activities with friends, family, and schoolmates. Happy types of quiet are shown, in addition to ones that result from naughtiness and nervousness. Pencil drawings colored digitally show wonderful texture and great facial expressions. Teachers, librarians, and parents may imagine an immediate use for this book, and it should work; the calming rhythm of the words and soft colors are soothing enough to settle most everyone.

Wayland, April Halprin   **5–9 YEARS**

NEW YEAR AT THE PIER:
A ROSH HASHANAH STORY
Illustrated by Stéphane Jorisch
New York: Dial, 2009 | 978-0-8037-3279-7

Izzy prepares for a modern-day Jewish New Year by making a list of what he is sorry for. On that day, he walks down to the pier with his family, the rabbi, the cantor, and other families. With his list in mind, Izzy says "I'm sorry" to those he has wronged. Izzy is a likable character who has done some things that any child could relate to. With ink, watercolor, and gouache artwork featuring Jorisch's distinctive figures, the story provides a good explanation of this Jewish holiday and some of the traditions surrounding it—especially *tashlich*, the casting away of wrongdoing. Izzy, his sister, his mother, classmates, and members of the congregation participate in the rituals of Rosh Hashanah in a book that melds lightheartedness with thoughtful reckoning. A good source for the study of other cultures and religions, this would also be an excellent choice for a discussion of friendship.

Whelan, Gloria   **6–10 YEARS**

YATANDOU
Illustrated by Peter Sylvada
Chelsea, MI: Sleeping Bear, 2007 | 978-1-58536-211-0

A young girl in Mali relates, in first person, how she helped the women of her village afford a millet-grinding machine. While her mother sells food products at the market, Yatandou sells the goat she has nursed from the time he was a runt. The new machine eliminates hours of pounding grain each day; it also brings the opportunity to learn from a teacher how to read and write. This highly affecting story is matched by expressive illustrations that capture the heat and hard work of the village people, especially Yatandou's family. (See figure 3.1.) An excellent portrayal of a very different life for children.

Figure 3.1 *Yatandou*

Yang, Belle   **5–9 YEARS**
HANNAH IS MY NAME
Illustrated by Belle Yang
Cambridge, MA: Candlewick, 2004 | 978-0-7636-2223-7

Hannah's story is an excellent explanation of green cards for young children. Coming to America from Taiwan with her mother and father, Hannah must learn a new language and wait for what seems like forever for the coveted green cards to arrive. Gouache illustrations in bold colors portray Hannah in her new apartment, at school, and at the diner where her father works. She wears red in every scene, symbolic of good fortune in Chinese culture. Endpapers in the front show the family in Taiwan with an ox-driven cart and, in the back, in a taxi in San Francisco, their new home. Set in the late 1960s, this story transcends time with its perfect capture of a young child's interpretation of events.

······ Friends ······

Bailey, Linda   **4–8 YEARS**
STANLEY'S WILD RIDE
Illustrated by Bill Slavin
Toronto: Kids Can, 2006 | 978-1-55337-960-7

Dreams of escape from his boring backyard come true for Stanley the dog, who leads his canine friends on a noisy night of fun. Busted! Delivered home by the police, Stanley goes meekly back to his yard—sort of. The acrylic artwork humorously portrays Stanley and the various breeds of his friends, the manner in which the dogs escape, and their rides in rolling forms of transportation. With dramatic page turns, a sentence begins on one page and continues on the next, while the tension ratchets up. The text does a marvelous job of capturing the excited sense of freedom and of describing an item by its look or smell, just as dogs would. For example, the skateboard is never named, just described as a "thing," but the illustrations show it very clearly. This is one of Stanley's many adventures with his friends, all of them comical and full of mischief.

Blumenthal, Deborah   **4–8 YEARS**
BLACK DIAMOND & BLAKE
Illustrated by Miles Hyman
New York: Alfred A. Knopf, 2009 | 978-0-375-84003-6

Because he can no longer win, a racehorse retires to a prison, where he becomes part of a horse care program. There he meets Blake, who is in prison for stealing to support his siblings and sick father. Although told in third person, the text makes clear Black Diamond's feelings of pride, pain, sadness, and, finally, affection for Blake. Color choices in the dry pastel illustrations—soft gold, brown, and orange—enhance this tender look at the human-animal bond. The setting appears to be the 1930s, lending a nostalgic feel. Each illustration, whether on one page or across two, is framed in a black line and kept entirely within that space, which fits well with the prison setting. Budding equestrians may also enjoy *Out of the Deeps* (Orca, 2008), another story of a horse in a unique setting—in this case, a coal mine.

Clark, Emma Chichester   4–8 YEARS
WILL AND SQUILL
Illustrated by Emma Chichester Clark
Minneapolis: Carolrhoda, 2006 | 978-1-57505-936-5

Originally published in England, this story delights in the use of language and picture as it follows the developing friendship of a young boy and a squirrel. The rhyme-loving Will and Squill even develop their own language. Colorful illustrations—with green dominating because most scenes take place outdoors—feature a variety of sizes: one full page alternating with two scenes on a page, with text interspersed among all. This placement makes the story fast moving as it packs in all the activities that Will and Squill share. Conflict occurs when Will's parents give him a kitten. He enjoys it for a while but then finds that he prefers Squill's company. Parallel situations, echo dialogue, and matching text make the prose lyrical.

Czekaj, Jef   4–8 YEARS
HIP & HOP, DON'T STOP!
Illustrated by Jef Czekaj
New York: Hyperion/Disney, 2010 | 978-1-4231-1664-6

Hip, a turtle who lives in Slowjamz Swamp, and Hop, a rabbit who makes her home in Breakbeat Meadow, love to create rhyming raps. But Hip's extremely slow raps put his audience to sleep, and Hop's fast ones cannot be understood. They meet while preparing for a rap concert and decide to work together. Instructions at the beginning of this story tell the reader at what speed to read the color-coded rhymes, either fast or slow, which should prove amusing to listeners. The comic-style art, featuring dialogue balloons, funny animals, and references to popular culture, complement the subject nicely. Hip and Hop learn to blend their styles and also encourage the other animals to join in the dancing, which provides a positive ending to this story.

Egan, Tim
ROASTED PEANUTS

Illustrated by Tim Egan
Boston: Houghton Mifflin, 2006 | 978-0-618-33718-7

The title gives a clue as to what is going to be important in this baseball story. Although Sam and Jackson like to think that they will someday play together in the big leagues, they both know that Sam is a natural athlete, good at all aspects of baseball, whereas Jackson can only throw. Looking out for and encouraging each other, Sam makes the team and Jackson becomes a peanut vendor known for his many-rows-over tosses. With a cast of animal characters, and Sam as a horse and Jackson as a cat, this story nevertheless is a study of human nature, with its joys and its disappointments, sweetened by loyalty and true friendship. Ink-and-watercolor illustrations feature tall Sam and squat Jackson, plus an assortment of pigs, cows, dogs, and others at the baseball field and in the neighborhood. Subdued humor and likable characters make this story a championship read.

Espinosa, Laura
OTIS AND RAE AND
THE GRUMBLING SPLUNK

Illustrated by Leo Espinosa
Boston: Houghton Mifflin, 2008 | 978-0-618-98206-6

Bold bright colors in blue, pink, and orange will catch the eye initially, and the story of two friends on a campout who meet a friendly monster will continue the attraction. Uncomplicated comical illustrations in a graphic novel style—some panels, dialogue balloons, lines around heads indicating strong emotions—are rendered in a mix of pencil, coffee, gouache, and Photoshop. Brave Rae and scared Otis make a good pair as they get into and out of several situations, none too scary for the younger crowd. The splunk is not too frightening, either, but he does emit a great grumble, which holds excellent possibilities for a read-aloud session.

Fleming, Denise
BUSTER

Illustrated by Denise Fleming
New York: Henry Holt, 2003 | 978-0-8050-6279-3

Isn't it common knowledge that dogs and cats don't care for each other? Buster, the title dog, leads a pretty good life until his owner, Brown Shoes, brings home Betty, a cat. Buster displays his emotions in both illustrations and text here: his fear, which causes him to stiffen; his studied nonchalance as Betty takes over his favorite things; his anger when she goes too far and changes his favorite radio station. Fleming shows

Figure 3.2 *Buster*

Buster's exuberance as he escapes to a beautiful park, then his increasing panic as he tries to find his way back home. Isn't it perfect that Betty, up in a tree, leads him back? The deep-hued illustrations, made by "pouring colored cotton fiber through hand-cut stencils," according to the illustration information, appeal in their color and textured look. (See figure 3.2.) A map that illustrates Buster's path from the park back home will delight map readers who like to follow along. In a further adventure, *Buster Goes to Cowboy Camp* (Holt, 2008).

Frazee, Marla   **4–8 YEARS**

A COUPLE OF BOYS HAVE
THE BEST WEEK EVER

Illustrated by Marla Frazee
Orlando: Harcourt, 2008 | 978-0-15-206020-6

Frazee provides a perfect example of a picture book where the illustrations convey the opposite of the text, providing loads of laughs. James and Eamon are the boys of the title, and their best week involves nature camp. Eamon's grandparents, Pam and Bill, babysit the boys when they are not at camp and supply lots of food (Pam) and information on penguins (Bill). The black Prismacolor-and-gouache illustrations take up most of each page, with the text hand-lettered. This book is just plain fun, and many listeners will think it is the best book ever.

Gorbachev, Valeri   **3–8 YEARS**

WHAT'S THE BIG IDEA, MOLLY?

Illustrated by Valeri Gorbachev
New York: Philomel/Penguin, 2010 | 978-0-399-25428-4

The "big idea" of the title is one that friends each try to generate as they think of a present for another friend's birthday. Molly the mouse, along with Rabbit, Goose, Frog, and Pig, all devise ideas that are too similar, until Molly has an inspiration. Even though some lines of text and pictures feature the secondary characters, Molly is the center of the story. The only named character, she unifies and leads the group. Lovely illustrations in watercolor, gouache, and ink provide an idealistic atmosphere of friends who cooperate and work together to surprise their friend Turtle. This book would be useful in explaining the creative process, for units on friendship or cooperation, or just as a gentle read-aloud.

Hopkinson, Deborah   **4–8 YEARS**

ABE LINCOLN CROSSES A CREEK:
A TALL, THIN TALE

Illustrated by John Hendrix
New York: Schwartz & Wade, 2008 | 978-0-375-83768-5

A story of friendship and daring starring Lincoln as a seven-year-old is an imaginative takeoff on two real characters—Abe and Austin—in 1816 Kentucky. Austin saves his friend from drowning when Abe falls off a log into a creek. Told in an aw-shucks manner, as if relating the tale around a campfire, the story crackles with danger and suspense. The author sometimes speaks directly to the audience, asking them to clap and call encouragement. At times, she refers to the artist, whose hand shows itself on several pages sketching and painting. This removal of the wall between author and reader contributes even more to the participatory storytelling feel. With their size and immediacy, the illustrations, in watercolor and pen and ink, invite readers and listeners to become involved in the story. The endpapers again show the illustrator's hand, sketches in black and white, broken pencils, and a sharpener, plus wadded-up paper. Making a character in history relatable to twenty-first century children is tough, but this book excels at it.

Howe, James   **4–8 YEARS**
HORACE AND MORRIS SAY CHEESE (WHICH MAKES DOLORES SNEEZE!)
Illustrated by Amy Walrod
New York: Ginee Seo/Atheneum, 2009 | 978-0-689-83940-5

When cheese-loving Dolores runs up against an allergy that makes her break out in itchy spots, the unthinkable happens. Under doctor's orders to stop eating cheese, Dolores finds herself obsessed with the food, and she is tempted to try some cheese again, which promptly makes her break out. The upcoming Everything Cheese Festival brings out her creative side, however, and she finds a way to indulge her love of food and cooking, albeit without cheese. This tale of three friends combines humor, dialogue, and situations. The love of cheese runs through the trio's adventures in other books, but this book puts it center stage. The acrylic illustrations enhance the text's humor and add their own—for example, Dolores's X-ray with perfectly formed cheese swimming inside her, or the movie posters full of "cheesy" humor. This story could be used for children who have a particular food allergy, but it would make a fun read-aloud for any group, with its kid-friendly story and art and its heroine overcoming an obstacle.

Jeffers, Oliver   **3–8 YEARS**
LOST AND FOUND
Illustrated by Oliver Jeffers
New York: Philomel/Penguin, 2005 | 978-0-399-24503-9

Disarmingly simple, this saga of a boy and a penguin celebrates friendship. With good intentions, the boy decides to return the lost penguin to the South Pole, but he finds that the bird is not happy there, just lonely. Eventually they row back home. The illustrations, as understated as the narrative, reflect what is going on in the text but add more attitude and humor. Jeffers depicts the journey to the South Pole impressively, with full-page spreads of water and sky and, eventually, ice floes. Illustrations of the two main characters show that the boy is only slightly bigger than the penguin, emphasizing their equality and their friendship. This beautiful story is perfect for read-alouds, parent-child sharing, or independent reading.

Keller, Holly **4–8 YEARS**
HELP! A STORY OF FRIENDSHIP
Illustrated by Holly Keller
New York: Greenwillow/HarperCollins, 2007 | 978-0-06-123913-7

Eye-catching illustrations combine with a story of mistaken interpretation. When Mouse expresses fear that Snake is out to hurt him, his friends Hedgehog, Squirrel, and Rabbit help him to see that it is not true. The unique art—collographs and water-colors—portrays what could be described as simply leaves and animals on each page, but the amazing detail of line and color makes it so much more. Keller explains her process of collographs (printed collages) on the inside back cover of the book jacket. The size and clarity of the illustrations make this a perfect read-aloud for groups. One of the page spreads will have to be rotated as it depicts a tall scene, making for variety. The story is perfect in its simplicity and clarity of theme.

McCarty, Peter **3–7 YEARS**
HONDO AND FABIAN
Illustrated by Peter McCarty
New York: Henry Holt, 2002 | 978-0-8050-6352-3

Hondo the dog and Fabian the cat, who live in the same house, go their separate ways one day for adventures. While Hondo enjoys a car ride and a frolic on the beach, Fabian stays home and plays with the baby and the toilet tissue. Fine illustrations, pencil on watercolor paper, enhance the story and its gentleness. Each two-page spread features an illustration on one page and text on the opposite. Soft, muted hues contribute to the unruffled feeling, as do the rounded bodies of the two main charac-ters. Animal lovers will delight in certain of the pictures, and even those who are not will be entranced by the baby picking up the cat or Hondo sprawled out on the floor asleep. The two continue their adventures in *Fabian Escapes*.

Noyes, Deborah **4–8 YEARS**
PRUDENCE & MOXIE:
A TALE OF MISMATCHED FRIENDS
Illustrated by AnnaLaura Cantone
Boston: Houghton Mifflin Harcourt, 2009 | 978-0-618-41607-3

True to their names, Prudence is careful while Moxie never heard a dare she did not try. Despite their differences, the two enjoy a good friendship, although Prudence is sometimes exasperated by Moxie. In only one case does the fearless Moxie quaver: she will not get anywhere close to Prudence's horse. The illustrations, rendered in mixed media, acrylic, and collage, project a goofiness that all ages will enjoy. Bright colors, patterned borders, and the wonderful antlers on Prudence and tail on Moxie attract the eye and satisfy the funny bone. The text, very realistic in its portrayal of friends and kid situations, has its own touches of humor, especially in the levels of "dare you" and in some of the harebrained activities Moxie attempts. A good match of word and picture, this story shows how everyone needs both a little prudence and a little moxie in their lives.

Numeroff, Laura   4–8 YEARS
WOULD I TRADE MY PARENTS?
Illustrated by James Bernardin
New York: Abrams, 2009 | 978-0-8109-0637-2

A young boy enjoys the time he spends at friends' houses, where he notices how the parents differ from his own. Even though his parents don't let him drink chocolate milk or have a pet, he knows he would not want to be in any other family. The boy appears with unruly hair and big glasses, adding a touch of goofiness to the illustrations rendered in acrylics and a digital paint program. The text does a good job of putting him in the shoes of his friends, great for young listeners who are just beginning to learn to look at the world from a point of view other than their own.

Perkins, Lynne Rae   4–8 YEARS
THE CARDBOARD PIANO
Illustrated by Lynne Rae Perkins
New York: Greenwillow/HarperCollins, 2008 | 978-0-06-154265-7

Best friends Debbie and Tina love to do amazing things. But when Debbie tries to find a way that Tina can practice the piano, it does not quite work out the way she wishes. Illustrations in watercolor and ink support the narrative and add details to it. Dialogue balloons showing alternating conversations appear in some scenes. Perkins captures perfectly the dynamic between two friends where one is more aggressive than the other, but where they work out their differences and preserve the friendship. The contrast between the two girls in looks and temperament shines through in the boldly colored illustrations. Smaller scenes, with two to four on a page, are interspersed with full-page illustrations, almost all roughly bordered with lots of white space. These friends strive to be amazing, and while their activities may seem normal, their imaginations make them remarkable. Readers will love them for that.

Robbins, Jacqui   **4–7 YEARS**
TWO OF A KIND
Illustrated by Matt Phelan
New York: Atheneum, 2009 | 978-1-4169-2437-1

Unfortunately, mean girls do not exist only in the upper grades; they start early. In this realistic school story, Kayla and Melanie torment Julisa and Anna. Told from Anna's point of view, this story shows how best friends can be separated by the manipulation of others. Watercolor illustrations provide the muted scenes of school life, with splashes of color in clothing. The facial expressions of both the mean girls and the good girls come through as realistic and moving. The fun and sharing of best friends, as well as the joy they take in learning, is palpable. The ethnic diversity of each pair of girls reflects the larger classroom. Readers and listeners will root for Anna and Julisa as they finally reunite and Anna realizes that Kayla and Melanie's attention is insincere. A great discussion starter on bullies, friendship, and being true to one's self.

Ryan, Candace   **3–8 YEARS**
RIBBIT RABBIT
Illustrated by Mike Lowery
New York: Walker/ Bloomsbury, 2011 | 978-0-8027-2180-8

With a sense of fun and a playful attitude toward language, this story of a frog and a bunny offers a realistic portrayal of friendship. The good times when they share and the bad times when they fight come through in text that includes rhymes and invented words and in illustrations that mirror this sensibility. The cartoon-style artwork employs pencil, traditional screen printing, and print gocco and is finished digitally. Although the friends fight over a robot, which provides the conflict of the plot, they reconcile in the end and return to being best friends. A deceptively simple story of friendship, this book explores conflict, loneliness, reconciliation, and the pleasures of sharing.

Sarcone-Roach, Julia   **4–8 YEARS**
THE SECRET PLAN
Illustrated by Julia Sarcone-Roach
New York: Alfred A. Knopf, 2009 | 978-0-375-95858-8 | library binding

Because they feel their mothers' interruptions undermine their playtime, an elephant and three cats (in side-by-side houses) conspire to make a plan to thwart bedtime. Acrylic paint illustrations in rich hues detail the living quarters and games of the friends: building a house of cards, constructing a tin can telephone, and making a fort out of cushions. The animals act just like children do, and reflect the childhood desire to prolong playtime. The fact that they live next to each other provides opportunities for illustration showing both houses at once. In fact, the endpapers at the beginning of the book show an architect's drawing of the houses, while those at the end show the house at night, surrounded by Morse code, which plays a part in the ending of the book. Clever, sweet, and funny, this story sneaks up on little cat feet, then makes a big impression.

Segal, John   **3–8 YEARS**
THE LONELY MOOSE
Illustrated by John Segal
New York: Hyperion, 2007 | 978-1-4231-0173-4

Two misfits come together to form a friendship: a hermit moose and a bird who cannot fly. The rather cranky moose comes to appreciate the singing, worm-eating bird. After a forest fire, the bird disappears. But never fear; a happy ending is in store when the bird returns in the spring and brings back many more birds. The spare illustrations depict the openness and enormity of a mountain setting. The scenes of night and of the fire are scary, but not overly so. The drawings project a gently humorous ambience and end with a dash of whimsy.

Sís, Peter   **4–8 YEARS**
MADLENKA SOCCER STAR
Illustrated by Peter Sís
New York: Frances Foster/Farrar Straus Giroux, 2010 | 978-0-374-34702-4

As in his other books, *Madlenka* (2000) and *Madlenka's Dog* (2002), Sís shows Madlenka and her block in the city containing her apartment building. In this outing, she loves to play soccer and finds a way to imaginatively interact with inanimate objects, animals, and, finally, friends. Madlenka is constantly on the move in the illustrations, usually facing to the right to show forward action and energy with each turn of the page. A sense of a child's place in her world permeates the Madlenka titles. Some of the illustrations feature a bird's-eye view from the top of her block, with a soccer field in the center, placing her and her neighbors in their environs. The endpapers, too, reflect this Earth-country-city-neighborhood-home connection. Illustrations with tiny flags of different countries and with children of varied backgrounds show the universal appeal of this sport. The final page spread provides a short history of soccer, plus the word *soccer* in forty-three different languages. For children who love soccer or sports or for a fun neighborhood story, *Madlenka Soccer Star* scores.

Soto, Gary   5–9 YEARS
CHATO GOES CRUISIN'
Illustrated by Susan Guevara
New York: G.P. Putnam's Sons, 2005 | 978-0-1424-0810-0

Chato, that low-riding cat of *Chato's Kitchen* (1995) and *Chato and the Party Animals* (2000), wins a cruise for two in this outing. He and his cat friend, Novio Boy, arrive at the ship and find it full of dogs. Disgusted by the food, games, and even the books in the ship's library (all about dogs), the two nevertheless try to have fun until all the dogs become sick and they must go for help. Acrylic on scratchboard illustrations depict wild and colorful scenes; the rowboat ride in the storm is particularly impressive. Black-and-white comic strips supplement with additional story, dialogue, and humor. Chato and Novio Boy are quite a pair of fun-loving cats, but they also illustrate the importance of keeping a promise when they give their word. A glossary at the end defines the Spanish words that appear throughout the text.

Willems, Mo   3–8 YEARS
CITY DOG, COUNTRY FROG
Illustrated by Jon J. Muth
New York: Hyperion/Disney, 2010 | 978-1-4231-0300-4

Beautiful in its simplicity and message, this story of friendship and change blends text and illustration perfectly. The dog meets the frog in the spring, they teach each other their country and city games throughout spring and summer, and eventually the dog finds himself alone in the winter. Each two-page spread features the text on one side and a full-page watercolor illustration on the other. Combining realism and humor, energy and passivity, joy and sorrow, the story represents the cycle of life. A very moving yet unsentimental way to explain death, the book also celebrates life and the glories of having a friend who understands. Each season's illustrations fill the pages with the colors and vegetation of that time of year. Compare with another fictional look at the life cycle of an animal, *Old Mother Bear* (Chronicle, 2007) by Victoria Miles.

······ SCHOOL ······

Anderson, Laurie Halse   5–9 YEARS
THE HAIR OF ZOE FLEEFENBACHER GOES TO SCHOOL
Illustrated by Ard Hoyt. New York: Simon & Schuster, 2009 | 978-0-689-85809-3

Zoe has big hair—really big hair. Its tendrils act as arms and its ends as fingers. It can even be a blanket or a sail. Trouble brews when Zoe's first-grade teacher, Ms. Trisk, states that she does not believe in wild hair. Humorous illustrations in watercolor and ink feature Zoe's orange hair, which takes center stage on almost every page. Note the contrast between the kindergarten teacher—in capris and a T-shirt—who loved Zoe's hair, with Ms. Trisk in her dark suit and tie. Readers and listeners will giggle over Ms. Trisk's attempts to control the hair, which really does function as a character in the story. All ends well as Zoe and Ms. Trisk and the hair find a way to coexist. And the teacher even loses her buttoned-up look; by the last page, she's in a polka-dot dress and sandals, with a lock of hair waving in the air.

Boelts, Maribeth   4–8 YEARS
THOSE SHOES
Illustrated by Noah Z. Jones
Cambridge, MA: Candlewick, 2007 | 978-0-7636-2499-6

To be a kid wanting the shoes seen in advertisements, the shoes all the kids at school are wearing, the shoes that cost too much—this story makes that yearning palpable. Jeremy, a young African American boy who lives with his grandmother, cannot believe his luck when he finds those shoes at a thrift store. He is willing to put up with their wrong size rather than wear the babyish shoes the guidance counselor gives him. But through his hurt and his observation of another classmate—the one who did not laugh at his Velcro shoes—he finds the courage to be generous. The illustrations are rendered in watercolor, pencils, and ink and assembled digitally. The affecting text expands with a variety of facial expressions and body language illustrating envy, anger, resignation, and excitement. Jeremy and his classmates present a slice of modern life.

Bottner, Barbara   4–8 YEARS
MISS BROOKS LOVES BOOKS! (AND I DON'T)
Illustrated by Michael Emberley
New York: Alfred A. Knopf, 2010 | 978-0-375-84682-3

From the first page, where the school librarian sits surrounded by piles of books, to the last, where she helps a student pick out a book from the library shelves, this story celebrates the joy of reading and the truth of "for every reader, a book." A young girl, unenthusiastic about reading, witnesses the love that Miss Brooks has for books and the many ways she tries to pass that love on to the students—through costumes, literature-sharing events, and book selection. Illustrated in pencil, ink, and watercolor, Miss Brooks and her exciting library activities show through in comic style. So, too, does the attitude of the girl who is irritated by all this emphasis on books . . . until the day she finds the book that appeals to her. A great read for any book celebration, this story stars quirky characters whose personalities shine through in text and artwork.

For another take on the love of books, see *Dog Loves Books* (Alfred A. Knopf, 2010) by Louise Yates.

Brennan, Eileen   **4–8 YEARS**
DIRTBALL PETE
Illustrated by Eileen Brennan
New York: Random House, 2010 | 978-0-375-83425-7

Cleaning up the normally dirty Pete presents quite a challenge for his mother, but it must be done. He has a speech to give at the school program honoring the fifty states. Representing Pennsylvania, Pete turns out quite well after a scrubbing and stays that way . . . for a little while. Filthy Pete, clean Pete, and costumed Pete appear in humorous cartoon-style illustrations along with Mom, armed for (scrubbing) battle, Pete's partner-in-grime dog, and his classmates. Although he reverts back to his dirt-smudged appearance, Pete makes the program special, and not just because of the way he looks. Both children and the adults who read to them will appreciate the humor in word and picture throughout this story. And they will applaud for Pete, even with garbage caught in his hair, just as the audience does at the school program.

Cocca-Leffler, Maryann   **4–8 YEARS**
JACK'S TALENT
Illustrated by Maryann Cocca-Leffler
New York: Farrar Straus Giroux, 2007 | 978-0-374-33681-3

For all those who do not think they are special, this book celebrates the fact that everyone possesses a talent. As the children in the class state their names and what they are good at, brightly colored artwork shows them enjoying these activities. But Jack cannot think of anything that he performs well, until the teacher hears him rattle off all the students' names and talents. And there it is: remembering is a talent, too. With bright colors, appealing characters, and a variety of activities from spelling to bug catching to singing, this book will act as reassurance and perhaps inspire tolerance. Pair this with David Conway's *Errol and His Extraordinary Nose* (Holiday House, 2010), where a small elephant discovers his talent among the other animals in his school.

Cotten, Cynthia   **4–9 YEARS**
ABBIE IN STITCHES
Illustrated by Beth Peck
New York: Farrar Straus Giroux, 2006 | 978-0-374-30004-3

Although she would rather read than stitch, Abbie must take needlework lessons to become an accomplished seamstress in 1822 New York State. As she struggles to learn the many stitches and to keep them straight and neat, she is overshadowed by her older sister, Sarah, who does it all so well and enjoys it. Abbie struggles to find a picture to stitch on her sampler and eventually finds one that will show her independent spirit. Impressionistic illustrations show Abbie and other girls studying stitching with Mrs. Brown, Abbie and her family, and Abbie reading. A good supplemental source for social studies, this book will educate children about a time in history when life was different from their own. An afterword provides a full page of information on samplers, needlework schools, and the life of girls in the 1800s.

Henkes, Kevin   **4–8 YEARS**
LILLY'S BIG DAY
Illustrated by Kevin Henkes
New York: Greenwillow/HarperCollins, 2006 | 978-0-06-074236-2

Lilly, who first appeared in Henkes' *Chester's Way* (HarperCollins, 1988), appears here as her teacher prepares for his wedding. Never one for self-doubt, Lilly is positive that she will be the flower girl for the wedding. Finding out that she will not have that honor, but that it is going to his niece Ginger, dampens her enthusiasm only slightly. As it turns out, all of her practice comes in handy when Ginger freezes. The characters, all mice, appeal with their charm and expressiveness. Many scenes are laugh-out-loud funny, such as Lilly making her bear dressed as her teacher spend time in the Uncooperative Chair. The watercolor illustrations invite the eye with their candy colors enhanced with black pen. Lilly may be stubborn and strong-willed, sometimes skating right on the edge of obnoxiousness, but her heart is in the right place.

Jenkins, Emily   **4–8 YEARS**
DAFFODIL, CROCODILE
Illustrated by Tomek Bogacki
New York: Frances Foster/Farrar Straus Giroux, 2007 | 978-0-374-39944-3

Triplets named after flowers: Daffodil, Violet, and Rose. Sounds cute, right? Apparently only to outsiders. Daffodil becomes fed up with teachers and classmates not able to tell her from her sisters. When her mother makes a crocodile head in an art class, Daffodil claims it as her own and wears it at home and at school. As a crocodile, she does whatever she wants and acts meanly. Daffodil's frustration comes through clearly in the text, matched by the cartoon-like illustrations. Sharp-eyed readers will find that the triplets are always dressed in shades of yellow, purple, and red, although not always matching their names of Daffodil, Violet, and Rose. Their home also contains vases of daffodils, providing a contrast to Daffodil's feelings of being overlooked. Children will relate to the way Daffodil's personality changes while she is wearing the crocodile head and reveling in the power it gives her, but they will also appreciate the safety of the ending, when the head has to be abandoned. The triplets' first adventure appears in *Daffodil* (Farrar Straus Giroux, 2004).

Noble, Trinka Hakes   4–8 YEARS
THE ORANGE SHOES
Illustrated by Doris Ettlinger
Chelsea, MI: Sleeping Bear, 2007 | 978-1-58536-277-6

Poverty and art come together in this story of a young girl who goes barefoot to school and who longs for pretty shoes like those of her classmates. When her teacher announces that the class will have a Shoebox Social, Delly decorates the box that her new shoes come in, ones that she thought her parents would never be able to afford. When the shoes are scuffed and stepped on by her classmates, she decorates her shoes to match the box. The illustrations bring out a range of emotions, including Delly's shame and hurt feelings, her happiness in having new shoes, her sadness when they are ruined, and her pride in her artistic triumph. Though not explicitly stated, the clothing styles and desks indicate a Depression-era setting.

Perl, Erica S.   3–7 YEARS
DOTTY
Illustrated by Julia Denos
New York: Abrams, 2010 | 978-0-8109-8962-7

A celebration of imaginary friends, this story features a very large and spotted creature that is Ida's constant companion. At school she meets other children and their imaginary friends. With sensitivity and realism, the author handles the matter-of-fact acknowledgment of Ida's classmates' imaginary friends, the point at which many are giving them up, and the embarrassment of having to ignore one's imaginary friend when others tease. Illustrations rendered in brush ink and Photoshop feature children with an almost manga look, plus some fantastic imaginary creatures. Ida's way of managing her feelings will resonate with children, and the encounter with her teacher at the end of the story will bring a sense of comfort and acceptance, as well as surprise. Pair with Patricia Polacco's *Emma Kate* (Philomel, 2005), whose imaginary friend is an elephant.

Piven, Hanoch   **4–8 YEARS**
MY BEST FRIEND IS AS SHARP AS A PENCIL: AND OTHER FUNNY CLASSROOM PORTRAITS
Illustrated by Hanoch Piven
New York: Schwartz & Wade/Random House, 2010 | 978-0-375-85338-8

The endpapers give a first clue that the illustrations in this book may be different: a jumble of colorful magnetic letters, pencils, blocks, and much more scatter over the spread. The story consists of a young girl describing her teachers and friends at school with similes; then the turn of the page features that person's illustration created with some of the objects that are in the endpaper photographs. The result is colorful and creative (who would have thought of a microscope for a nose?). Gouache is also used in the illustrations. A fun inspiration for a lesson in portraits in art class, this book could also be used in language arts and writing.

Prelutsky, Jack, compiler   **5–10 YEARS**
THERE'S NO PLACE LIKE SCHOOL
Illustrated by Jane Manning
New York: Greenwillow/HarperCollins, 2010 | 978-0-06-082338-2

A collection of eighteen poems, this book covers everything: taking off for school in the morning, riding the bus, recess, lunch, hallway antics, and even homework. Many of the poems are humorous, even the ones that involve some mildly alarming topics, such as not being ready for a test or not knowing the answer when called upon. Poet Prelutsky gathers an entertaining selection here, with two by himself and verses by twelve other poets. The watercolor illustrations feature children and teachers in a comical bent, to match the text. Poem titles stand out in brightly colored letters, matching the color palette of the illustrations. Perfect for poetry lovers, for use in language arts classes, and for teachers who want to experience the sheer joy of presenting poetry as it should be—read aloud.

Primavera, Elise   **4–8 YEARS**
LOUISE THE BIG CHEESE
Illustrated by Diane Goode
New York: Paula Wiseman/Simon & Schuster, 2009 | 978-1-4169-7180-1

Louise yearns to be a diva with every fiber of her being, but she remains a likable character despite her run-ins with her parents, sister, and best friend. The possibility of playing Cinderella in the school play brings out her extra-wattage star ambitions. The text, supplemented by balloon dialogue, expresses her wishes and her actions. Watercolor illustrations match the text and add attitude in delightful cartoon-style art, heavy on the pink. Notice the contrast between Louise's rather plain parents and the look-alike houses on her block compared to Louise's room and her dreams of Broadway stardom. The book concludes with a quiz to test the reader's potential for becoming a star. Endpapers present "Big Cheeses throughout History" and "Little Cheeses throughout History," another humorous contrast piece. Louise carries on her diva ways in *Louise the Big Cheese and the La-Di-Da Shoes* (Simon & Schuster, 2010).

Recorvits, Helen   **4–8 YEARS**
YOON AND THE JADE BRACELET
Illustrated by Gabi Swiatkowska
New York: Frances Foster/Farrar Straus Giroux, 2008 | 978-0-374-38689-4

The author captures perfectly the feelings of childhood, especially the longing for friendship, the shame of doing something wrong, and the joy of overcoming obstacles. An older girl at school tricks Yoon, a recent immigrant from Korea, into giving up her family heirloom bracelet. Impressionistic illustrations capture the various moods: wanting to be invited to play jump rope, gratitude at receiving the bracelet, frustration in attempting to get it back, and relief at being aided by a kind teacher. Backgrounds, richly textured, sometimes contain wallpaper-like designs that mirror the colors and designs of the dresses. A fine tale of the immigrant experience in America for young children, this story is told in first person, which lends an intimate feel. Meet Yoon in *My Name is Yoon* (Farrar Straus Giroux, 2003) and *Yoon and the Christmas Mitten* (Farrar Straus Giroux, 2006).

Rodman, Mary Ann   **4–7 YEARS**
FIRST GRADE STINKS!
Illustrated by Beth Spiegel
Atlanta: Peachtree, 2006 | 978-1-56145-377-1

Haley begins the new school year in first grade but finds out quickly and to her disappointment that everything about it is different from kindergarten. The teacher is more subdued, the classroom is not decorated, there is only one recess, and on and on. Even with the help of her friend Ryan, Haley has difficulty accepting this and finally has a meltdown. When she finds that her teacher understands her, she begins to appreciate all the things about first grade that are better than kindergarten. The text expertly captures a first grader's mind-set, while watercolor-and-ink illustrations show kindergartners and first graders in all their silliness, joyousness, frustration, and happiness. The small size of Haley as she enters her new classroom reveals how overwhelmed she feels in this new environment. The picture of her outburst, when she yells out the title of the book, shows her as very big indeed. First graders will delight in this story whether they recognize themselves or not, and younger ones will see what is coming.

Rubel, Nicole   3–7 YEARS
HAM AND PICKLES: FIRST DAY OF SCHOOL
Illustrated by Nicole Rubel
Orlando: Harcourt, 2006 | 978-0-15-205039-9

Children who experience jitters on the first day of school may be comforted by this humorous look at the problem. Little Pickles has a thousand and one worries about school, manifested in continuous questions aimed at her older brother, Ham. From getting up on time to wearing the right clothes to finding her classroom, Pickles frets about everything, and Ham tries to allay her fears. Several of his suggestions inspire humorously illustrated scenes, although his words are matter-of-fact; in other cases, both are funny. The illustrations, rendered in ink, markers, colored pencils, crayons, and collage items, pack each page with details. Listeners may want to search for items and identify photographed pieces. Readers familiar with Rubel's illustrations for the Rotten Ralph series will recognize the similar goofy humor.

Rumford, James   4–8 YEARS
RAIN SCHOOL
Illustrated by James Rumford
Boston: Houghton Mifflin Harcourt, 2010 | 978-0-547-24307-8

The first day of school in a village in the country of Chad brings a lesson for Thomas, who is attending for the first time. The children must build the school, and so they do, learning to make bricks, walls, and desks from the mud, and a roof from grass and sticks. School finally starts, and they learn to read and write. As the school year ends, rains come and the cycle of the year begins again. Vivid and textured illustrations show the joy of learning, always with a background in shades of brown and tan that portray the earth from which the school is literally made. A look at school life in another country for young listeners first encountering cultural and geographic differences, Rumford's story is based on his experiences in Chad as a Peace Corps volunteer.

Russo, Marisabina   4–8 YEARS
A VERY BIG BUNNY
Illustrated by Marisabina Russo
New York: Schwartz & Wade/Random House, 2010 | 978-0-375-84463-8

For those who feel they don't fit in, this book presents an encouraging story of acceptance. Amelia, the big bunny of the title, towers over most of her classmates, who will not play with her. She spends much of her time entertaining herself, until Susannah, the new bunny in class and the smallest, befriends her. At first resistant, Amelia is won over by Susannah's persistence and creativity. Colorful gouache art shows bunnies of all sizes and colors in the classroom and on the playground. A gentle story about being different, this book portrays meanness and kindness realistically.

Watt, Mélanie   **4–7 YEARS**

AUGUSTINE

Illustrated by Mélanie Watt
Toronto: Kids Can, 2006 | 978-1-55337-885-3

Although the main character is a penguin, this story readily transfers to all human children who have ever had to move or to start a new school in the middle of the year. As Augustine and his parents relocate from the South Pole to the North Pole, he goes through all the steps of packing, saying good-bye, and moving into a new home. At his new school, Augustine endures some awkward times but then becomes friends with classmates through his art. The book pays tribute to famous painters, some of whose masterpieces inspire Watt's illustrations. Each two-page spread features one page divided into nine squares, each containing one of these paintings and then other objects that add detail to the text on the facing page. The text includes some clever wordplay and in-jokes that probably only the adults will catch. In any case, all will be enchanted by the appealing characters, the crisp colors rendered in acrylic and pencil crayon, and the universal experience of trying to fit in.

Williams, Karen Lynn, and Khadra Mohammed   **5–10 YEARS**

MY NAME IS SANGOEL

Illustrated by Catherine Stock
Grand Rapids, MI: Eerdmans, 2009 | 978-0-8028-5307-3

A look at the immigrant experience, this story follows a young boy from a refugee camp in Africa to a new home in America. Besides adjustments to the weather and a new school, he finds that no one in this new country can pronounce his name. Finally he comes up with an idea inspired by his soccer team shirt. The expressive art illustrates the crowded confusion of an airport, the family's apartment so different from their old home, and the colorful classroom filled with new faces. A young boy's problem and his solution will inspire students.

Winters, Kay   **4–8 YEARS**

THIS SCHOOL YEAR WILL BE THE BEST!

Illustrated by Renée Andriani
New York: Dutton/Penguin, 2010 | 978-0-525-42275-4

With the enthusiasm of the title, the children of this story express their hopes for the coming school year. They share both practical and fanciful wishes that most children could relate to. The illustrations feature a diverse group, in both gender and ethnicity, inhabiting the classroom, playing field, and their own homes as they imagine soccer goals, out-of-this-world field trips, and snow days. The cartoon-style artwork bursts with fun and activity and ends with the whole group holding up drawings of their hopes. This is an ideal book for the first day or week of school.

4

Out in the World

The picture books in this section move the story outside the circle of family, friends, and school into the wider world. Readers will encounter new cultural experiences, recognizing that everyone is a global citizen. They will also develop an awareness of history and a sense of continuity by learning that others came before.

Alalou, Elizabeth, and Ali Alalou   4–8 YEARS
THE BUTTER MAN
Illustrated by Julie Klear Essakalli
Watertown, MA: Charlesbridge, 2008 | 978-1-58089-127-1

The authors evoke the keenness of hunger and the satisfaction of satiety, which become the underlying conflict in this story. A young girl's *baba*—her father— tells about his childhood while he prepares an evening meal of couscous. Travel to Morocco in this story within a story, where his mother finds a way to take her young son's mind off their lack of food by telling him to wait for the butter man. Full-page gouache illustrations face each page of text, the colors reflecting the landscape of a drought-stricken country. (See figure 4.1.) The font size of the first line of text in the book is larger, as it is in the first line of the story that Baba tells and in the return to the present day, signaling these changes in time and perspective. An author's note and glossary assist with understanding the geography and culture of the High Atlas Mountains of Morocco.

Figure 4.1   *The Butter Man*

Alexander, Cecil   3–7 YEARS
ALL THINGS BRIGHT AND BEAUTIFUL
Illustrated by Ashley Bryan
New York: Atheneum/Simon & Schuster, 2010 | 978-1-4169-8939-4

The century-old hymn of the title provides the majestic words illustrated by stunning collage art. Bryan used his mother's sewing and embroidery scissors to cut the brightly colored papers that take the shape of people, animals, and objects in this book. Layering the pieces creates the depth; delicate cuts give texture to the compositions. Each page provides an abundance to look at, either by one reader or in a group. Art teachers may want to use this as a preliminary read before embarking on older students' construction paper collages; inventive ideas for portraying water, wind, people, and vegetation abound in this beautiful book.

Applegate, Katherine
THE BUFFALO STORM
Illustrated by Jan Ormerod
New York: Clarion, 2007 | 978-0-618-53597-2 | library binding

The storm of the title refers to both thunderstorms, which scare young Hallie, and the storm of buffalo hooves as they thunder across the prairie. She deals with each as she travels west with her parents to Oregon in a covered wagon. The text, in first person, stays true to a young girl's feelings as she leaves her beloved grandmother and faces the challenges of a long journey. Watercolor-and-pastel illustrations also capture the emotions of the characters and offer some exciting scenes, especially when Hallie falls out of the covered wagon and when she rescues a buffalo calf. The double-page spread of the running of the buffalo herd pulses with power and strength; the dust that surely obscured them in real life shadows over the great brown shapes. A strong female character who overcomes fears and worries shines through in this pioneer story. Partner this with Jean van Leeuwen's *Papa and the Pioneer Quilt* (Dial, 2007).

Arnosky, Jim
4–8 YEARS
GRANDFATHER BUFFALO
Illustrated by Jim Arnosky
New York: G.P. Putnam's Sons, 2006 | 978-0-399-24169-7

Follow along on the migration of a buffalo herd as it traverses the prairie, and see the role the old buffalo takes on as protector of a newborn calf. Combining fiction and nonfiction allows the story to present facts about this magnificent animal and the cycle of life while concentrating on the engaging story of one character. Large watercolor illustrations capture the colors of the landscape and the times of day as well as the great brown animals. Especially dramatic is the transition from a long view on one page to a close-up of the buffalo's face that completely fills the next page. Listeners should look carefully on each page for other, smaller animals that appear. Ideal for group read-alouds, this book would be a perfect supplement to science or social studies curricula. The text, forthright yet moving, combines with realistic illustrations to provide a wonderful introduction to a piece of the American past.

Avi
5–10 YEARS
SILENT MOVIE
Illustrated by C. B. Mordan
New York: Anne Schwartz/Atheneum, 2003 | 978-0-689-84145-3

Reflecting an important part of its plot, this book is structured as a silent movie: in black and white, with frames of action and with limited phrases to give needed information. Incredibly detailed ink on clayboard illustrations play up the melodramatic mood of the story, which concerns an immigrant family from Sweden and their trials and triumphs in New York City. Partner this with some Charlie Chaplin, Buster Keaton, or Harold Lloyd movies, especially with older children. The author's and illustrator's notes present a personal look at the creative process behind this unique book.

Barasch, Lynne   4–9 YEARS
FIRST COME THE ZEBRA
Illustrated by Lynne Barasch
New York: Lee & Low, 2009 | 978-1-60060-365-5

Parallel stories take place in this book about cooperation and friendship. One story involves the zebra, wildebeest, and gazelle that share the grazing lands in Kenya. The first few pages illustrate how each animal eats only the top, middle, or lowest sections of the grass. The other, more personal story features two boys. Abaani, of the nomadic Maasai people, cares for his family's cattle, while Haki, a Kikuyu boy, helps his family sell the vegetables grown on their farm. At first the boys yell hateful phrases at each other, words they have heard from others in their tribes. But one day, they come together to rescue a baby from angry warthogs and so begin a tentative walk toward friendship. By the end of the book, they talk, play games, and trade vegetables for milk. Recalling the beginning, the ending compares the boys' sharing to the animals' sharing of the grass; thus there is hope for the future. The ink-and-watercolor illustrations depict the grasslands, cattle pens, and roads of the Kenyan countryside, as well as the people and animals. An author's note concludes the book with more information about the Maasai, the Kikuyu, their rivalry, and the game of mancala that the boys play. A glossary with pronunciations is included for unfamiliar words and phrases.

Bauer, Marion Dane   4–8 YEARS
THE LONGEST NIGHT
Illustrated by Ted Lewin
New York: Holiday House, 2009 | 978-0-8234-2054-4

With a quiet sense of anticipation, this book portrays the cold darkness deep in the forest, where the animals await the coming of morning. Watercolor illustrations, which reveal the largeness and wildness of the animals, consist of dark blue, green-blue, and brown until the last five pages. As the sun comes up, pale pink and yellow filter through the branches as the transition to daylight becomes complete. The text presents as a prose poem, with the crow, moose, and fox offering to find the hiding sun and wake it up. But finally it is the tiny chickadee that brings the sun back. Young readers and listeners will love the large, up-close illustrations of the forest animals.

Bildner, Phil   **4–8 YEARS**

THE HALLELUJAH FLIGHT
Illustrated by John Holyfield
New York: G.P. Putnam's Sons/Penguin, 2010 | 978-0-399-24789-7

When aviator James Banning and mechanic Thomas Allen flew across the United States from Los Angeles to New York in 1932, they encountered ridicule, mechanical difficulties, bad weather, and prejudice. For they were the first African Americans to make a transcontinental flight. Illustrations that capture the emotions of the main characters give this story its personal feel within the context of history. The text brings forth their determination in the face of many obstacles, as well as the adventurous spirit that kept them going. The book puts readers in the seat of that early aircraft to make them feel the heat and the wind, to see the scenery of America, to feel hunger when they were not allowed to eat in restaurants, and to hear each other call "Hallelujah" whenever they made a good landing. This fictionalized version about real people and a real event will introduce Banning and Allen to children for whom this story will be an inspiration and a high-flying adventure.

Blake, Robert J.   **6–9 YEARS**

SWIFT
Illustrated by Robert J. Blake
New York: Philomel/Penguin, 2007 | 978-0-399-23383-8

Looking for heart-pounding action? This story, set in the wilderness of Alaska, brings it on—with intensity. A bear attacks a boy and his father. Pa, with a broken leg, sends Johnnie and his dog, Swift, off for help. A snowstorm, a fall in a river, and that now-wounded bear are just a few of the terrors they must face. Realistic oil paint illustrations capture the forest and tundra, as well as the pain, cold, and fear. Endpapers showing the routes taken by Pa and Johnnie will appeal to listeners who enjoy maps. Those who oppose hunting may not be able to get past the scenes of both the boy and his father with guns, but those who are willing to accept this reality of the setting will find a story of faithfulness, growing up, and the human-animal bond. The author's note at the end recounts his experience with, and information about, homesteading families in Alaska.

Brown, Peter   **4–8 YEARS**

THE CURIOUS GARDEN
Illustrated by Peter Brown
New York: Little, Brown, 2009 | 978-0-316-01547-9

Imagine going from a smoky and drab cityscape to a green and flowery one. That progression happens from the first page spread to the last in this story of Liam, who decides to take care of a few plants. He starts small, watering and pruning the sad specimens on an abandoned railroad track. But soon the garden spreads, and eventually other people join in and transform the city. The illustrations, acrylic and gouache, range from small, quarter-page, and unframed, to multiple framed illustrations on a page, to full two-page spreads. Several pages show the expansion of the garden with illustration only. The text, quiet and matter-of-fact, reflects Liam's personality. The illustrations add information, such as Liam singing to his plants, which is not explicitly stated in the text. The change of seasons occurs, and even winter keeps the hero of the story busy with plans for planting in the spring. Brown adds a touch of whimsy with the illustrations of topiary animal shapes. A must-read for gardeners and conservationists who hope to pass on their love of growing things to a younger generation.

Bunting, Eve   5–8 YEARS
POP'S BRIDGE
Illustrated by C. F. Payne
Orlando: Harcourt, 2006 | 978-0-15-204773-3

This book takes a fictional look at historical fact—the building of the Golden Gate Bridge—witnessed through the eyes of a young boy whose father works on its construction. He and his friend, Charlie Shu, whose father is a painter on the bridge, observe its construction, a terrible accident, and its completion while watching over their fathers with binoculars. The illustrations, full one- and two-page spreads, show both the scenes of the huge project and the up-close emotions of the boys. The faces of these characters, plus others in crowd scenes, offer fascinating detail, capturing the feel of the 1930s. The first-person text perfectly blends the personal—a son's pride, worry, and elation—with the big picture. Fascinating perspectives, such as the reflection of the bridge in the binoculars in one such scene, make the illustrations noteworthy. A note from the author with further information about the construction of the bridge concludes the book.

Chen, Jiang Hong   5–10 YEARS
LITTLE EAGLE
Translated by Claudia Zoe Bedrick
Illustrated by Chen Jiang Hong
New York: Enchanted Lion, 2007 | 978-1-59270-071-4

First published in France, this captivating book takes readers to China, where Master Yang rescues an abandoned orphan. Lyrical storytelling combines with magnificent illustration as the young boy discovers that his guardian is a master of eagle boxing, a form of kung fu. The boy becomes Little Eagle, training with the master for years. Gorgeous art depicts all phases of his life; an especially evocative series over two pages displays the exercises he performs during each of the four seasons, each in a different hue. As the master ages and the two enter into battle with their enemy, the action peaks. It ends as one generation passes on to the next. The large size of the book makes it a natural for reading aloud, although children who are into any of the martial arts will enjoy paging through it on their own. Follow the real eagle throughout the book, his presence a symbol of courage and discipline.

Connor, Leslie   **4–9 YEARS**
MISS BRIDIE CHOSE A SHOVEL
Illustrated by Mary Azarian
Boston: Houghton Mifflin, 2004 | 978-0-618-30564-3

Beautiful woodcut illustrations lend an old-fashioned feel to this fictional story of a young woman who leaves her home in 1856, travels to a new land by boat, and builds a life for herself, all with the help of a shovel. The cover illustration portrays the title character setting off with shovel in hand, and every illustration throughout the book includes the shovel. Each illustration is bordered in black, with the text outside of the border or, in some cases, in a black-bordered box within the illustration containing and picking up the black outlines of the woodcuts. This book could be used as supplementary material in social studies, with its scenes of life from the second half of the nineteenth century. Emigration, a woman's life span from teenager to grandmother, rural living, love and loss—all these themes combine in this rich story.

Conway, David   **4–8 YEARS**
LILA AND THE SECRET OF RAIN
Illustrated by Jude Daly
London: Frances Lincoln, 2008 | 978-1-84507-407-4

Readers and listeners will almost feel the heat of the atmosphere in this story, in which a Kenyan village teeters on the verge of drought. Lila worries, especially after hearing her mother talk about consequences of no rain, so she consults with her grandfather. Acting on a story he relates, she climbs to the top of a mountain and begins to tell the saddest things she knows. With a welcome onset of rain, the people of her village celebrate. Dry-dust browns dominate the illustrations, with a large golden sun in the daytime pictures. The reader views the scenes as if from far off, enhancing the feel that this takes place far away. Stories told by the grandfather and Lila appear in gray with splashes of red, providing a contrast to the warm colors of the majority of the illustrations. The text, beautiful in language, gathers the reader in and makes the ending believable. In combination with the art, it becomes a total package that will transport listeners to the African desert.

Cooper, Elisha   **4–9 YEARS**
BEACH
Illustrated by Elisha Cooper
New York: Orchard/Scholastic, 2006 | 978-0-439-68785-0

Interesting perspectives make this illustrated story of a day at the beach memorable. Taking the long view, the artist shows the beach gradually filling with people at the beginning and emptying out at the end. In between, small watercolor-and-pencil illustrations, sometimes more than two dozen to a page, illustrate sunbathers, swimmers, animals, clouds, boats, and more in what is almost a sketchbook of all that an artist can observe. It is as if that artist were sitting on a hill looking at the beach and painting, giving a *plein air* feeling. While the drawings exhibit an undetailed, almost unfinished look, they go well with the text, which is detailed in its observations, except for a few pages that are wordless. The large-size format of the book affords plenty of room for all the illustrations, lots to look at, and a good size for sharing with a group.

Cooper, Ilene   **6–9 YEARS**
THE GOLDEN RULE
Illustrated by Gabi Swiatkowska
New York: Abrams, 2007 | 978-0-8109-0960-1

All the major faith traditions follow some version of the Golden Rule, and in this story, a young boy, in talking with his grandfather, discovers what this is and how to put it into practice. Impressionistic illustrations incorporating the symbols of various faiths provide a thoughtful and rich visual experience. Drawings of angels, animals, Hindu gods, Madonna and child, and decorative elements surround the boy and his grandfather. Especially moving is their dialogue about war, when soldiers and knights and airplanes in moody black-and-white sketches fill the two-page spread. A wonderfully evocative introduction to this concept for the young. Christian, Jewish, Islamic, Hindu, Buddhist, and Native American forms of the Golden Rule are included.

Da Costa, Deborah   **6–10 YEARS**
SNOW IN JERUSALEM
Illustrated by Cornelius Van Wright and Ying-Hwa Hu
Morton Grove, IL: Albert Whitman, 2001 | 978-0-8075-7525-3 | paper

Avi, a young boy who lives in the Jewish quarter, and Hamudi, a young boy of the Muslim quarter, both believe that a white cat who occasionally visits belongs to him alone. When Avi follows the cat one day, he discovers Hamudi, and the two boys argue about ownership of the animal. A rare snow in their city leads them to follow the suddenly missing cat, and they track down her kittens. Muted colors with rich textures capture the streets of Jerusalem and two of its quarters. Note the realistic facial expressions of the boys. An author's note provides more information about the city of Jerusalem and its inhabitants. A glossary lists pronunciations and definitions for the Hebrew and Arabic words in the text. This beautifully told and illustrated story serves as an introduction to this part of the world and as a story about problem solving.

Ehlert, Lois   **4–8 YEARS**
LEAF MAN
Illustrated by Lois Ehlert
Orlando: Harcourt, 2005 | 978-0-15-205304-8

From the forms of the leaves to the colors and shapes of the pages, this book presents a complete package of the wonders of fall leaves. In Ehlert's author's note, she describes her passion for collecting leaves from all over; color copies of them became the illustrations. Her clever positioning turns them into chickens and pumpkins, cows and carrots, as well as the Leaf Man. Exquisite textures and sumptuous colors of orange, gold, brown, and green take the reader into a fall day no matter what the weather outside. The upper edges of the pages, die-cut into scallops and scoops and zigzags, create the mountains, meadows, forests, and rivers of the story setting. The text flows, matching the ever-moving course of the book and the floating Leaf Man. A unique and lovely book to fall into.

Elliott, David   **4–8 YEARS**
IN THE WILD
Illustrated by Holly Meade
Somerville, MA: Candlewick, 2010 | 978-0-7636-4497-0

A collection of poems, each focused on one animal, make up this gorgeously illustrated picture book. The animals represent many habitats and continents, from the lion that begins the book to the polar bear that ends it. Each two-page spread features one animal and its poem, which ranges from four lines to thirteen. The illustrations—woodblock prints and watercolor—depict the animals large and in motion for the most part. The physical size of the book makes it ideal for sharing in a group setting. A wonderful cross-curricular source, this book could be used in science, language arts classes studying poetry, and nature studies. It is also sure to be a favorite for students who want to look at it on their own and enjoy the beauty of the art and the animals.

Evans, Freddi Williams   **5–9 YEARS**
HUSH HARBOR: PRAYING IN SECRET
Illustrated by Erin Bennett Banks
Minneapolis: Carolrhoda, 2008　|　978-0-8225-7965-6　|　library binding

Secret meeting locations where African American slaves can worship as they please, free from the eyes of their overseers, become places of refuge and hope in this story. A young boy is deemed old enough to be entrusted as lookout during worship. Through his eyes and ears, readers and listeners see the fieldwork, listen to the old stories, discover a runaway, and hear the singing and prayers for freedom. Expressionistic illustrations in rich browns, greens, and reds convey the experiences of young Simmy and the other slaves. The text focuses on characters, such as Uncle Sol, Simmy's mother, and Mama Aku, giving a personal touch to history. With its compelling story and informational author's note, this book would be an excellent supplementary source for social studies. *Hush Harbor* offers an affecting look at the religious life of slaves, which is not usually covered in picture books as thoroughly as other aspects of their lives.

Fern, Tracey E.   **4–9 YEARS**
BUFFALO MUSIC
Illustrated by Lauren Castillo
New York: Clarion, 2008　|　978-0-618-72341-6

From late nineteenth-century Texas comes this historical fiction based on a real pioneer woman who took in orphaned baby buffalo, nursed them to health and maturity, and eventually sent them off to national parks and wildlife refuges. Told in first person, the story reveals Molly's motivation for saving buffalo clearly and with a bit of humor. The illustrations depict the hard work of farming and ranching, the devastation of the buffalo kills, and the heartwarming appearance of the buffalo calves. An author's note provides information on Mary Ann Goodnight, the real woman behind the story, plus sources for further information.

Fleming, Candace   **5–9 YEARS**
BOXES FOR KATJE
Illustrated by Stacey Dressen-McQueen
New York: Melanie Kroupa/Farrar Straus Giroux, 2003　|　978-0-374-30922-0

Based on events in post–World War II Europe, this story captures the excitement and gratitude of a Dutch girl receiving a box containing soap, socks, and chocolate from young Rosie in Indiana. A correspondence between the two ensues, and more boxes arrive for Katje and the cold and hungry people of her town. Exuberant illustrations depict the emotions of the characters; insets of square illustrations, often with hand-written letters, look like photographs that convey what is happening on both sides of the Atlantic. The pages become fuller as the story proceeds, reflecting the bigger, more numerous boxes and the explosion of Rosie's project to include many other people in her town who want to help. The ending, in which the Dutch people send tulip bulbs to their American friends, is just perfect.

Fletcher, Susan   **6–10 YEARS**
DADBLAMED UNION ARMY COW
Illustrated by Kimberly Bulcken Root
Cambridge, MA: Candlewick, 2007 | 978-0-7636-2263-3

A combination of the serious and the lighthearted, this story puts a fictional spin on the historical cow that traveled with the Union Army. During the Civil War, a young man enlists and his cow follows him through marches and battles and even his hospital stay. Although a lot of trouble, she also provides milk and winter warmth to the soldiers. Pencil-and-watercolor illustrations do this cow justice: she and the men show a wide range of emotions in the variety of situations pictured. An author's note concludes the book with information about the real cow. And just to remind readers who the most important character is, a painted expanse of textured cowhide makes up the endpapers.

Franco, Betsy   **3–7 YEARS**
BIRDSONGS
Illustrated by Steve Jenkins
New York: Margaret K. McElderry/Simon & Schuster, 2007 | 978-0-689-87777-3

A book about birds. A counting book. A wonderful example of collage illustration. All these descriptions suit *Birdsongs,* which is framed by the rising of the sun at the beginning to its setting at the end. In between, readers meet ten different species of birds, each of which fills the page—either singly or in a flock—and which voices (in written words) its distinctive sound. The text of these coos and caws and quacks surround and in some cases cover the birds, in a different font size and usually in a different color from the main text. In descending order from ten to one, these sound words and the birds spread over each set of two pages accompanied by a tree, a nest, a feeder, or other habitat. At the end, after the sun sets, the mockingbird appears to mimic the other birdcalls, all of which appear on the page around her. A concluding section called "Feathery Facts" presents information about the birds shown. Large illustrations, full of color and texture—as well as the possibility of some creative sounds—make this ideal for a read-aloud.

Frank, John   **6+ YEARS**
HOW TO CATCH A FISH
Illustrated by Peter Sylvada
New Milford, CT: Neal Porter/Roaring Brook, 2007 | 978-1-59643-163-8

From Tobago to Florida, from Ireland to Japan, fishing takes a variety of forms in this collection of poems, which visits thirteen places in all. The words express beautifully the techniques for catching fish, usually a certain type of fish, and in a very up-close manner; the reader or listener will feel as if he or she is right there. The illustrations in impressionistic style match the beauty of the text. The colors include more than the expected blue or green of the sea; colors of sunrise and sunset, plus reds in clothes and lighthouse also appear. Each picture is labeled with the type of fishing depicted (ice fishing, surf casting, spearfishing, dip-netting, etc.) and the place where it occurs. The book concludes with a child and father fishing, a nice personal touch.

George, Jean Craighead   **4–8 YEARS**
THE LAST POLAR BEAR
Illustrated by Wendell Minor
New York: Laura Geringer/HarperCollins, 2009 | 978-0-06- 124067-6

Writer George and illustrator Minor, both prolific in their fields, take readers to the Arctic in this story that combines a dreamlike encounter and the stark realism of climate change. Young Tigluk meets a polar bear that seems to want him to follow her. With his grandmother's help, Tigluk journeys to a remote area of the Arctic Ocean, where he discovers what the mother bear wanted him to find. Beautifully textured artwork depicts the blue-white of snowy skies, the yellow-gray of the polar bear, and different colors of the ocean. The double-page spreads of the ocean journey present moving scenes: Tigluk and his grandmother paddling their kayak in a sunset-orange ocean, a huge walrus with a baby on the shore of a blue sea with pink and yellow sky, and a large polar bear head peeking out of the green water. Beautifully rendered visuals combine with a text that blends an exciting story and timely message.

Graber, Janet   **4–8 YEARS**
MUKTAR AND THE CAMELS
Illustrated by Scott Mack
New York: Christy Ottaviano/Henry Holt, 2009 | 978-0-8050-7834-3

This book will transport most children to a completely foreign place, both geographically and in life experience. A young boy, a refugee from Somalia, lives in an orphanage in Kenya. He and the other children go to school, yet he often dreams of his former life with his parents and the camels that are so important to their lives as nomads. When a small caravan arrives at the orphanage with books for the school, Muktar finds that his skill working with an injured camel may fulfill his dream of tending camels. A moving story of a young boy, the text perfectly complements the illustrations, oils on canvas, that feature the boys of the orphanage, the teacher, and the camels. Shades of brown and yellow dominate, reflecting the color scheme of the desert, with splashes of red and blue in clothing. Muktar's dreams, done in shades of gray, lend an eerie atmosphere. Added features include a map of Africa, with Kenya and Somalia highlighted, and a brief author's note about these two countries, war, and the camels that deliver books.

Hegamin, Tonya Cherie   5–9 YEARS
MOST LOVED IN ALL THE WORLD
Illustrated by Cozbi A. Cabrera
Boston: Houghton Mifflin, 2009 | 978-0-618-41903-6

In this story about the use of quilts in the Underground Railroad, a little girl witnesses her mother sewing pieces together. Her mother explains what the squares mean and eventually sends her daughter off to freedom with the quilt around her. Rich illustrations, rendered in acrylic paint and textile collages, wonderfully express a little girl's curiosity and her mother's pain and hope. Many of the scenes are set against a dark background, reflecting the subject and the fact that much of the action takes place at night. The important quilt squares—the North Star, the log cabin, the tree with moss on the north side, and the little girl surrounded by a heart—depict easy symbols for young readers to understand, just as they were for the girl in the story. Don't miss the endpapers, which consist of pieced quilts. An extensive author's note and a list of books and websites for further reading close the book. Include with other books on quilts and slavery, such as Jacqueline Woodson's *Show Way* (Putnam's, 2005) and Deborah Hopkinson's *Under the Quilt of Night* (Anne Schwartz/Atheneum, 2001).

Hucke, Johannes   4–8 YEARS
PIP IN THE GRAND HOTEL
Illustrated by Daniel Müller
New York: NorthSouth, 2009 | 978-0-7358-2225-2

An excellent example of the action moving from left to right as the page turns, this story begins with a girl's pet mouse escaping from its box and into a fancy hotel. Brightly colored illustrations feature comical people and detailed settings. As the little mouse runs through the lobby, kitchen, pantry, and more, these crowded rooms supply numerous places for him to hide, and for readers and listeners to search for him. The large size of the book enables the illustrations to take up the bulk of the page, with the text appearing in a narrow strip at the bottom. Every page spread contains a sentence that needs to be completed by turning the page. This device keeps suspense high and the story moving. This seek-and-find book is not too complicated for a younger audience, and the story provides a behind-the-scenes look at a hotel with some agreeable companions. Originally published in Switzerland.

Levine, Ellen   **4–9 YEARS**
HENRY'S FREEDOM BOX
Illustrated by Kadir Nelson
New York: Scholastic, 2007 | 978-0-439-77733-9

Based on the true story of Henry "Box" Brown, this fictionalized version of his life examines his childhood and young adulthood and the factors that led to his remarkable plan to escape slavery. With the help of collaborators on both ends, he decided to mail himself in a box from Richmond, Virginia, to Philadelphia. His is a sad story, full of separation and loss, and it is told in a way that does not diminish this pain even as it is made understandable to children. Nelson creates haunting artwork, rendered in pencil, watercolor, and oil, expressive in detail and mood-defining use of color and texture. The series of drawings showing Henry in the box being shoved every which way by men on the boat jolts readers with its cross-section view. The contrast of lightness and darkness and use of color is stunning; compare the pages where he sees his family being sold versus the pages where he arrives in the box in Philadelphia. Supplement with another story of a male slave, who runs away aided by the Underground Railroad and his faithful dog, in Elisa Carbone's *Night Running* (Knopf, 2008).

Lofthouse, Liz   **4–10 YEARS**
ZIBA CAME ON A BOAT
Illustrated by Robert Ingpen
La Jolla, CA: Kane/Miller, 2007 | 978-1-933605-52-4

A young Afghan girl, en route to a new country and freedom, endures a crowded and at times frightening voyage over the sea. Cutting between that present-day experience and thoughts of the past, readers and listeners learn of Ziba's life in the mountains: playing and helping, observing her mother, listening to her father, and finally being driven away by violence. This spare text does not go into detail on the war, as it does with other experiences Ziba remembers, respecting the sensibilities and understanding of a child. Evocative illustrations depict the boat ride and Ziba's memories in richly colored and textured art. (See figure 4.2.) The people, especially faces, are particularly well portrayed. Because of the short length and the child-centered nature of the text, this book could be used to explain immigrant experiences to young children, yet it is deep enough even for adults.

Mansfield, Howard   **4–8 YEARS**
HOGWOOD STEPS OUT: A GOOD, GOOD PIG STORY
Illustrated by Barry Moser
New York: Neal Porter/Roaring Brook, 2008 | 978-1-59643-269-7

Can a six-hundred-pound behemoth of a pig be considered adorable? In this book, appealing illustrations, first-person (or would that be *first-pig*?) point of view, and a style that extols the elemental pleasures of dirt baths and vegetable gardens could convince anyone. The watercolor art is remarkably realistic in its depiction of animals, humans, and landscapes. As Hogwood escapes his pen and takes a trip through neighboring yards and gardens, he comments on what he feels, and he reacts to the neighbors and the policeman, who most certainly do not think he is a good pig. Hogwood's adventure is an excellent choice for classes studying farm animals, or just as a fun read-aloud. Grown-ups can read his story in *The Good Good Pig* (Ballantine, 2006) by Sy Montgomery, Mansfield's wife.

McClintock, Barbara   **4–8 YEARS**
ADÈLE & SIMON
Illustrated by Barbara McClintock
New York: Frances Foster/Farrar Straus Giroux, 2006 | 978-0-374-38044-1

Take a trip through Paris at the turn of the last century in this book featuring the delightful illustrations for which McClintock is known. Simon leaves school with his supplies and articles of clothing, which he loses one by one as he and his sister walk home. Each page turn reveals a new scene, including a market, garden, museum, Métro station, and more, which provide crowds of people and lots of places for Simon to lose things. Young readers will have fun finding the missing items in each picture. Adults may be more interested in the explanations at the end of the book about each scene and trying to identify some of the famous people who are part of the illustrations. Although not mentioned in the text, Miss Clavell and the little girls of *Madeline* appear in one of the pictures. Be sure to look at the endpapers, taken from a 1907 map. Continue the fun with *Adèle and Simon in America* (Frances Foster/Farrar Straus Giroux, 2008).

McCully, Emily Arnold   **4–9 YEARS**
WONDER HORSE
Illustrated by Emily Arnold McCully
New York: Henry Holt, 2010 | 978-0-8050-8793-2

Although the title character, named Jim Key, takes center stage in this story, equally important is Bill Key, the man who takes care of Jim and teaches him. A former slave,

Figure 4.2   *Ziba Came on a Boat*

94

Doc Bill uses his skills as a veterinarian to care for animals, always stressing that they must be treated with kindness. Jim Key, foal of Doc's favorite horse, seems to show an uncanny ability to unlock gates and find hidden objects. Over the years, Doc teaches Jim letters, numbers, and colors. Appealing illustrations take listeners through a range of emotions during the events of Doc's and Jim's lives. Based on a true story, this fictionalized version portrays Doc's affection for his horse and his struggle to have both academic experts and the Society for the Prevention of Cruelty to Animals recognize Jim's abilities. Illustrations portray the historical setting (Jim Key lived from 1889 to 1912), but are timeless in their portrayal of the human-animal bond.

McGinty, Alice B.   **4–8 YEARS**

THANK YOU, WORLD
Illustrated by Wendy Anderson Halperin
New York: Dial, 2007 | 978-0-8037-2705-2

Although children of different countries experience diverse living styles, they also encounter similar feelings and activities. The cover introduces the eight children who appear inside the book. Each two-page spread contains eight squares. Each square illustrates a scene from the United States, Mexico, Bolivia, France, Mali, Saudi Arabia, India, and China. The text, a unifying sentence that begins with "Thank you," addresses elements of nature, a swing, a window, and a mother that each square depicts. Children may want to go through this book page by page, looking at all the pictures at once, or looking at just one country's illustrations at a time. With eight on each spread, the pictures are small and intimate, reflecting the child and his or her everyday experiences therein. (See figure 4.3.) The illustrations, in crayon and pencil, can lead to discussions of differences and cultural traditions of each country, as well as similarities. The endpapers again consist of eight squares, each with a globe highlighting the country and its continent or hemisphere. A beautiful book and a springboard to cultural understanding.

McMullan, Kate   **3–8 YEARS**

I STINK!
Illustrated by Jim McMullan
New York: Joanna Cotler/HarperCollins, 2002 | 978-0-06-029849-4

With the vigor and loudness that only a large vehicle can muster, a garbage truck tells all. Since this garbage truck works at night, the illustrations emerge in shades of brown, gray, blue, and purple, with yellow illumination popping up occasionally. The text is in your face, with words—and sometimes individual letters within a word—appearing in differing font sizes. In the middle of the truck's trip, an A-to-Z listing of all types of nasty garbage turns up. Some of these will be sure to elicit laughs from

I'm dancing with the breeze.

Figure 4.3   *Thank You, World*

young listeners. The truck is anthropomorphized in the illustrations, a technique that fits well with the first-person text. Both words and pictures portray the roaring power of this necessary machinery. From the front cover, *I Stink!* comes on strong, all the way through to the back cover, which displays a smaller truck, eyes closed, smiling sweetly. Fans may want to check out the McMullans' *I'm Dirty!* (2006), about a backhoe, or *I'm Mighty!* (2003), featuring a tugboat, or, for dinosaur lovers, *I'm Bad!* (2008).

Ó Flatharta, Antoine   **4–8 YEARS**
HURRY AND THE MONARCH
Illustrated by Meilo So
New York: Alfred A. Knopf, 2005 | 978-0-375-83003-7

A fine example of combining nonfiction facts within a fictional story, this book portrays the migration of monarch butterflies through the story of one butterfly's journey and her fleeting acquaintance with a tortoise. This story spans October to the next spring, as it contrasts the short life of the traveling monarch and the seemingly unchanging life of the old tortoise. The beautiful watercolor art features close-ups of the two animals, as well as impressive groups of monarchs and the life cycle of egg to caterpillar to butterfly. On the endpapers, a map of North America indicates the migration of the monarchs from Canada to Mexico. An afterword provides more information and statistics about this amazing journey. Compare this with *Arabella Miller's Tiny Caterpillar* (Candlewick, 2008) by Clare Jarrett, and Anne Rockwell's *Becoming Butterflies* (Walker, 2002), with its school setting.

Pendziwol, Jean E.   **4–8 YEARS**
DAWN WATCH
Illustrated by Nicolas Debon
Toronto: Groundwood/Douglas & McIntyre, 2004 | 978-0-88899-512-4

The shimmering haziness of the illustrations reflects the setting of the story as a young girl helps her father keep watch during the night in a boat on Lake Superior. Language rich with imagery imparts information about sailing and the sea; the first-person narrative describes the emotions of the girl on watch. Hues of deep blue and black dominate the illustrations throughout most of the book, with several pages in green as the northern lights come into view, and then orange and yellow as day begins to dawn. The textured paintings take a variety of views: the boat tiny in a huge sea, the boat large with views of the equipment and people on board, scenes where the reader will feel present on the boat, and others as if looking down on it from above. The overall impression is of movement and cold and watchful waiting. Teachers may want to use this book as an example of descriptive writing before students undertake such an assignment, or for any water- or boat-themed storytime.

Pinkney, Andrea Davis   **4–8 YEARS**
PEGGONY-PO: A WHALE OF A TALE
Illustrated by Brian Pinkney
New York: Jump at the Sun/Hyperion, 2006 | 978-0-7868-1958-4

Moby Dick has nothing on Cetus, the sixty-ton whale who tries to escape pursuit by Galleon Keene and the wooden boy he carves, Peggony-Po. The Pinkneys have created a seafaring tale with elements of Pinocchio, exuberant in action on the ship and in the water. The young boy's fictional battle with the whale is set in the 1840s, a prime time for the whaling industry. Illustrations in rich colors portray the whale, the waves, the ship, and the people constantly moving, mimicking a ship-based journey. A rhyming sea chantey offers even more authenticity. The text highlights Peggony-Po's daring, a great adventure for young listeners. End material includes a note on whales and black whalers, plus a glossary of nautical terms.

Raschka, Chris   **4–8 YEARS**
LITTLE BLACK CROW
Illustrated by Chris Raschka
New York: Richard Jackson/Atheneum, 2010 | 978-0-689-84601-4

With beautiful use of line and color, the watercolor-and-ink illustrations in this story feature the crow of the title, who is indeed little in most of the art. The impressionist illustrations and the poetic text display the essence of the crow and his story. One could hand this book to an aspiring children's writer and say, "Here, this is how rhyming text is done superbly." The soft, lilting feeling of the book and its essence of nature, family, and love combine to create a deceptively simple look that hides deeper truths.

Ravishankar, Anushka   **4–8 YEARS**
ELEPHANTS NEVER FORGET!
Illustrated by Christiane Pieper
Boston: Houghton Mifflin, 2008 | 978-0-618-99784-8

Befitting its title character, this book contains some large and loud words. The noises of a lightning storm, tiger, buffalo, and elephant spread across the page in extra-big type to maximize the effect. The illustrations themselves, digitally created, consist of just three colors: black, blue, and light cream. Constant action—running and rolling, swimming and throwing—will appeal to short attention spans. The small size of the elephant on most pages emphasizes his feelings of being alone and not fitting in. The basic story, in which a little elephant separated from his herd finds a group of animals to live with, is simple but affecting. Originally published in India.

Roth, Susan L.   **4–8 YEARS**
GREAT BIG GUINEA PIGS
Illustrated by Susan L. Roth
New York: Bloomsbury, 2006 | 978-1-58234-724-0

The big guinea pigs of the title exist in a story that a mother guinea pig tells her little one. As she relates it, huge, sharp-toothed guinea pigs lived in swamps in Venezuela eight million years ago. A variety of papers from around the world, including basket weave, cellophane, and hand-marbled, make up the incredible collage illustrations. An extensive note about the art, found on the inside back flap, states the origins (countries and cities) of these materials. The modern-day guinea pigs embody cuteness and fluffiness, while the long-ago ones loom large and scary-looking. The scenes of the modern guinea pigs always contain the basket weave paper, emphasizing their home in a cage. The text provides facts, enhanced by the illustrations, but also contains humorous and innocent comments by the little guinea pig. A bibliography is included at the end. This book blends fiction and nonfiction exceedingly well for the very young.

Say, Allen   4–8 YEARS
THE BOY IN THE GARDEN
Illustrated by Allen Say
Boston: Houghton Mifflin/Houghton Mifflin Harcourt, 2010 | 978-0-547-21410-8

The book opens with a one-page story of the Grateful Crane, necessary background for the plot, since it is a story that the young boy knows well from his mother's telling. Jiro and his father pay a visit to a family friend who lives in a house with a large garden. While walking through the garden, Jiro discovers a statue of a crane that he at first believes is real. Hearing the adults gently laughing at him, he walks away, and from there this story takes on a dreamy quality. As in the story of the Grateful Crane, his experience includes a house, a woman coming in from a snowstorm, and the sound of a loom. On every page spread, the text appears on the left side and the watercolor illustration on the right. The real scenes are framed with a white border, while the fantasy scenes take up the whole page with no border. The transition from reality to fantasy occurs seamlessly and naturally, so it is a surprise to the reader when the father, looking for Jiro, wakes him from his dream. His words at the end assure his son that he was not foolish for thinking that the crane looked real. A gently magical story masterfully told, *The Boy in the Garden* exudes a sense of curiosity and wonder.

Scanlon, Liz Garton   3–7 YEARS
ALL THE WORLD
Illustrated by Marla Frazee
New York: Beach Lane/Simon & Schuster, 2009 | 978-1-4169-8580-8

Through rhythm and rhyme, the text gives the reader a picture of a summer day at the seashore, a farmers' market, a storm, a restaurant meal, and a family gathering. Its comfortable feeling of happiness and being in just the right place with loving family members permeates the story. Pencil-and-watercolor illustrations portray modern people, but a comfortable old-fashioned quality makes the pictures timeless. This is a wonderful book to share with a loved child or to read aloud to a group and revel in the rhythmic text. Children who like to pore over pictures for details will enjoy several double-page spreads. A good book for anyone, child or adult, who wants to feel part of something bigger.

Schertle, Alice   3–8 YEARS
LITTLE BLUE TRUCK
Illustrated by Jill McElmurry
Orlando: Harcourt, 2008 | 978-0-15-205661-2

With a rollicking rhythm and some mighty fine rhymes, this story of a truck in the country celebrates the animate (farm animals) and the inanimate (trucks). When a dump truck gets stuck in the mud, and the little blue truck gets stuck trying to help, the animals come to the rescue. Gouache illustrations feature the natural colors of farmland: brown, gold, yellow, and green. This makes Little Blue Truck stand out even more. The animals sport a comical look, and the trucks, with eyeball headlights, zip along humorously. No human beings are in evidence, even as drivers. Almost every page contains four lines of text with an *abab* rhyme scheme, an easy feel to read out loud, and an abundance of animal and truck noises. These "conversation" words—*beep*, *honk*, *oink*, *moo*—appear in color within the text. The same wonderful rhyme and rhythm, but transported to the city, take place in *Little Blue Truck Leads the Way* (Houghton Mifflin, 2009).

Schwartz, Howard   4–8 YEARS
GATHERING SPARKS
Illustrated by Kristina Swarner
New York: Roaring Brook/Holtzbrinck, 2010 | 978-1-59643-280-2

Lovely prose and illustrations combine in a story that gently encourages goodness in order to repair the world. Based on the Jewish tradition of *tikkun olam,* the explanation that the grandfather gives his granddaughter about the origin of stars and the purpose of humans is inspiring. Because the book is set for the most part at twilight and night, the colors, rich in shades of blue and purple, deepen as the story progresses. The color scheme also includes greens, which fit in with the environmental message, an important part of the story. This gentle book is full of affection and hope.

Stringer, Lauren   3–8 YEARS
WINTER IS THE WARMEST SEASON
Illustrated by Lauren Stringer
Orlando: Harcourt, 2006 | 978-0-15-204967-6

Although the title seems counter to the obvious cold of winter, this picture book explains why winter is warm, from a child's point of view. With warm clothing, animals hibernating in dens, and hot food as examples, the book makes the point easily. The illustrations, in acrylics, exude richness and warmth and follow through on the imagery of the text. Some illustrations show a contrast between summer and winter, such as the swimming pool and the bubble bath, but most show winter scenes filled with fun or cozy images of snowmen and hot chocolate and quilts. Recurring shapes of snow drifts, rounded and white, frame many of the illustrations. These round shapes match pictures of puffy jackets, melting cheese on a sandwich, and a curled-up cat. The text includes some internal rhymes and many image-laden words to provide its rhythm and flow. Teachers may want to use this when studying the seasons, while parents may want to do so for a warm and snug read-aloud.

Stryer, Andrea Stenn   4–8 YEARS
KAMI AND THE YAKS
Illustrated by Bert Dodson
Palo Alto, CA: Bay Otter, 2007 | 978-0-9778961-0-3

One of the delights of literature is its ability to take a person to a place he or she may never physically visit. This book transports readers to the Himalayan Mountains, where young Kami tracks down his family's missing yaks. When he discovers an injury among one of the flock, he must go for help just as a hailstorm begins. Because he is deaf and cannot talk, he must use sign to communicate what has happened to his father and older brother. Determined and resourceful, Kami serves as a role model for young children who feel as if they may be too young to make a difference. The illustrations, paintings with almost palpable texture, take the reader to this land of the Sherpas, with its mountains and snow. An author's note at the end of the story provides information on the life of the Sherpas, their work, families, and homes. Also set in the Himalayas and peopled with children in a Nepali guide family is Olga Cossi's *Pemba Sherpa* (Odyssey, 2009).

Wellington, Monica   3–7 YEARS
TRUCK DRIVER TOM
Illustrated by Monica Wellington
New York: Dutton, 2007 | 978-0-525-47831-7

With bright primary colors and simple illustrations of vehicles, people, and animals, this story follows a truck driver who carries a load of fruits and vegetables from a farm into a big city. Color copies of photographs pasted onto gouache art make an engaging combination of the realistic and painted. Curvy roads, train tracks, construction vehicles, bridges, and stores combine to fill the pages with details for young listeners to examine. At the end, an illustrated list of all forty-seven vehicles appears so that they can be found elsewhere in the book. Almost all the vehicles are very small; thus, many fit onto a page, and their progress along the roads can be shown. The simple language of the text, which may encourage early readers, is upbeat and active, reminiscent of classic Lois Lenski books such as *The Little Auto, The Little Fire Engine,* and *Papa Small.*

Winter, Jeanette   **4–8 YEARS**
ANGELINA'S ISLAND
Illustrated by Jeanette Winter
New York: Frances Foster/Farrar Straus Giroux, 2007 | 978-0-374-30349-5

A newcomer to New York City, Angelina misses her native Jamaica. She longs for the food, the weather, her school, the birds, and the old games; everything in her new home fades by comparison. Her mother discovers that Carnival is celebrated in Brooklyn and arranges to have a beautiful costume made for Angelina so that she can dance in the parade. Winter's illustrations burst with color throughout, even in her depictions of New York City, but the Carnival dance scenes really explode. Genuine and poignant feelings come through in the first-person text, supplemented by the illustrations that add a depth of emotion to what is expressed on each page. Teachers and parents may want to play some Jamaican music while reading this book.

Winter, Jonah   **4–9 YEARS**
HERE COMES THE GARBAGE BARGE!
Illustrated by Red Nose Studio
New York: Schwartz & Wade/Random House, 2010 | 978-0-375-85218-3

Based on the true story of the barge that hauled garbage from Long Island down the coast and failed to find a dumping ground, this fictionalized version combines fantastic illustrations with text that begs to be read aloud. Even for those listeners unfamiliar with the states and countries that were part of this event (a great opportunity for learning map skills), the story does a good job of depicting the geographic areas. The illustrations—photographs of hand-built, three-dimensional sets—invite close examination: strange characters, realistic machines, and lots and lots of garbage make them perfect for the almost subversive tone of the text. Regional dialects and phrases will be fun to read out loud. A unique story about a unique event, this book conveys an environmental message with savvy humor.

Winter, Jonah
4–9 YEARS
STEEL TOWN
Illustrated by Terry Widener
New York: Atheneum, 2008 | 978-1-4169-4081-4

From the title page spread, with its factories and billowing smoke, and throughout much of the book, a feeling of dark and damp permeates. Black, gray, and dark brown predominate, with flares of yellow and orange that capture the fire in the furnace. This acrylic art meshes beautifully with rhythmic text that describes what happens in a steel mill. A fine example of mixing fiction with nonfiction, this story oozes heat and fire, clanking machinery, and huge buildings. Set in a time of five-cent hot dogs and "Pennies from Heaven" on the radio, this tribute to ethnic families and their hard workers in a steel town shines through.

Would, Nick
5–9 YEARS
THE SCARAB'S SECRET
Illustrated by Christina Balit
New York: Walker, 2006 | 978-0-8027-9561-8

The sumptuous illustrations will draw readers in, and then the story takes off! And what a story it is—full of suspense, danger, and help from an unexpected source. Told from the point of view of a scarab beetle, the story takes place in ancient Egypt. Hidden in a basket of figs, this scarab is carried to a newly built tomb. There he discovers a stone slab set as a trap for the prince who comes to inspect the place. The action in the text moves quickly, and the illustrations, rich in Egyptian symbol and design, add a visual dimension that helps put everything in perspective. The beetle appears small in most of the pictures, so readers and listeners will have fun looking for it. Balit has beautifully depicted the tomb itself, with its doors and passageways and stone floors, as well as the costumes of the characters. An author's note at the end provides further information on the Egyptians and their tombs. Gorgeous visuals and a heart-pounding story make this an exciting adventure.

Yerxa, Leo
4–9 YEARS
ANCIENT THUNDER
Illustrated by Leo Yerxa
Toronto: Groundwood/House of Anansi, 2006 | 978-0-88899-746-3

Stunning illustrations featuring handmade paper that looks like leather make this book visually appealing throughout. Each painting of horses in watercolor and gouache is set upon a shirt or dress, inspired by traditional clothing of Native Americans of the Plains. With no more than nine words per page spread, the text captures the power of the horses whose hooves provide the thunder of the title. As these animals and others race across the pages and appear on the clothing depicted, they lend a feeling of power, majesty, swiftness, and color, to the story. A unique book, *Ancient Thunder* is an excellent source for the study of Native Americans, for art classes, for language arts and poetry, and for children who enjoy stories about horses.

Young, Ed   **4–9 YEARS**
HOOK
Illustrated by Ed Young
New York: Neal Porter/Roaring Brook, 2009 | 978-1-59643-363-2

With just a few words on each page and large illustrations, this book is a natural for group read-alouds. A young Native American boy discovers an egg in the forest and brings it home for his chicken to hatch. When the bird comes out with a distinctive beak, the boy names him Hook—and all seem to know that he is meant for flight. After watching several of Hook's failed attempts to fly, the young boy takes him to a canyon, where the bird finally takes off with wings spread wide. Brown and tan dominate the full-page illustrations, with shades of blues, greens, and reds for contrast. An almost solemn mood permeates the book; this is not a funny "Mother Hen hatches a strange egg" story. From the beginning, even the hen knows that this bird is meant for a higher purpose. The magnificent picture of Hook's flight at the end features his wingspan, which reaches from one corner diagonally across two pages to the other. This is an awe-inspiring story for animal lovers, budding conservationists, and those who want to hear stories of success.

5

The World of Imagination

I n the picture books in this section, anything can happen. Although impossible in real life, the stories take place in the fertile ground of the imaginative mind. Children can learn about real life through the stories, too, as characters or themes may be real even if situations are not. Silly or sweet, magical or mysterious, these books encourage the reader to think creatively.

Ahlberg, Allan   4–8 YEARS
THE PENCIL
Illustrated by Bruce Ingman
Cambridge, MA: Candlewick, 2008 | 978-0-7636-3894-8

This delightful story focuses on the illustrations, which are being drawn as the story progresses. The pencil of the title—the main character—draws a boy, a dog, a cat, and from there much, much more. The story begins in black and white (it's a pencil, remember?), then picks up color after the pencil draws a paintbrush. Conflict comes in the shape of an eraser! The humor is gentle and understated; for example, most of the characters insist on being named by the pencil. See the endpapers, where objects and their names are on display, such as a bridge named Ramona and a rug named Marcus. The acrylic illustrations underline the humor with their simplicity and child appeal. Readers and listeners familiar with *Harold and the Purple Crayon* by Crockett

Johnson will note the same self-referential theme, although *The Pencil* contains more characters and color. An excellent choice for artists young and old who believe in the power of the pencil and the pen—and the eraser. In a similar vein, read *Jeremy Draws a Monster* by Peter McCarty (Holt, 2009).

Baker, Keith   **3–7 YEARS**
LMNO PEAS
Illustrated by Keith Baker
New York: Beach Lane/Simon & Schuster, 2010 | 978-1-4169-9141-0

Here is an alphabet book starring, as the title promises, peas. More than just a green vegetable, these peas sport facial features, arms, and legs, as they ride bikes, play musical instruments, and perform science experiments, among many other activities. Each letter of the alphabet represents, and is surrounded by, peas of a certain occupation or peas engaged in activity; for example, hikers climb over the *H* and miners tunnel through the *M*. One to three of these jobs partner with each letter. Digital illustrations feature a large letter on each page, although some pages contain two letters and some letters take two pages. The little peas and their equipment go over, under, around, or through the letter. Touches of humor give a light mood to the book, as does the overall demeanor of the peas. The rhyming text flows along, with just a few words on each page; after a reading or two, young listeners will probably be able to identify what word comes next with a little prompting. Even for those who turn up their nose at eating peas, this ABC book is a delicious experience.

Barnett, Mac   **4–8 YEARS**
BILLY TWITTERS AND
HIS BLUE WHALE PROBLEM
Illustrated by Adam Rex
New York: Disney/Hyperion, 2009 | 978-0-7868-4958-1

In this hugely entertaining fantasy, a young boy acquires a weighty task: to take care of a blue whale. Told in the first person, the text contains statements that the illustrations humorously contradict. Adults reading this book will appreciate the sly humor; for example, the blue whale owner's manual mimics a foldout airline safety card, with its diagrams and arrows. In every scene in which Billy's parents appear, dialogue balloons cover them from the neck up, underscoring the pronouncements coming from faceless authority. The author cleverly sneaks in facts about the blue whale and dinosaurs, which take nothing away from the laugh-out-loud mood of the story. Endpapers feature old-fashioned ads for odd products having to do with the sea, keeping the silly mood going.

Barton, Chris   4–8 YEARS
SHARK VS. TRAIN
Illustrated by Tom Lichtenheld
New York: Little, Brown, 2010 | 978-0-316-00762-7

All hail the creative brains behind this book! One vigorous situation after another
spurs a battle between a shark and a train. Who would win if these anthropomorphized toys were pitted against each other in, say, a pie-eating contest or bowling? All
these settings are framed by two pages preceding the title page that depict two boys
digging through a toy box to find the shark and the train, and two pages at the end
that show the boys tossing their favorites back in the toy box before they run to lunch.
This story presents a perfect blend of word and picture, where the text presents the
situation and action-packed illustrations bring out the humor in over-the-top fashion.
Dialogue balloons provide even more sly humor, which will appeal to adults reading
the story as well as to the children listening. Look for the page that gives new meaning to the phrase "jump the shark" and an homage to its origins. For lovers of action,
comedy, ridiculous situations, and, of course, sharks and trains.

Black, Michael Ian   4–8 YEARS
A PIG PARADE IS A TERRIBLE IDEA
Illustrated by Kevin Hawkes
New York: Simon & Schuster, 2010 | 978-1-4169-7922-7

With droll humor in the text and laugh-inducing illustrations, this story asks that the
reader or listener use imagination and yet face cold reality. The imagined pig parade,
gloriously illustrated in acrylics featuring snappy uniforms, brilliant color, and even
fireworks, marches out cartoon-style pigs. Compare those to the realistic porcines
featured in the pages that explain why pigs will never march, dress in uniform, or
play band instruments. The close-up of the pig snout after snuffling along the street is
priceless! Children and the adults who read to them can enjoy this book on different
levels of humor and laugh together.

Broach, Elise   4–9 YEARS
WHEN DINOSAURS CAME
WITH EVERYTHING
Illustrated by David Small
New York: Atheneum, 2007 | 978-0-689-86922-8

For readers and listeners in search of pure fantasy of the "wouldn't it be great if . . ."
variety, this book is a real find. For every purchase, doctor's visit, and haircut, a child
receives a free dinosaur. Not the little plastic ones, but a real dinosaur. In the comical

illustrations of watercolor and ink, the little boy appears thrilled and store clerks and nurses unruffled; the only one who seems to be upset is the boy's mother. The dinos, of course, appear huge on each page where they are featured; on others, only their big heads are visible through windows. For those kids who are begging for a pet, this story offers a lot of parallels. (Did the hadrosaur *really* follow him home? Or did he tempt it with a doughnut?) Even Mom comes to terms with the dinosaurs in the end, and all live happily ever after. For more giant fun, see Laura Joy Rennert's *Buying, Training & Caring for Your Dinosaur*, a humorous list-type story.

Brown, Monica   4–8 YEARS
CHAVELA AND THE MAGIC BUBBLE
Illustrated by Magaly Morales
Boston: Clarion/Houghton Mifflin Harcourt, 2010 | 978-0-547-24197-5

Bountiful color bursts from the pages of this story, which combines facts about chicle with a fantastical journey through time. Chavela blows bubbles of all shapes and sizes, and when she finds some magic chicle at the store, she must have it. Her *abuelita*—her grandmother—tells her about her own father who was a *chiclero* in the rain forests. Soon Chavela blows a bubble with the magic chicle that takes her to Mexico, where she meets a little girl and other children playing near the chicle trees. The real magic is revealed when Chavela returns home and finds out that her *abuelita* was that little girl. Candy colors make up the full-page illustrations, rendered in acrylics. Certain words—*bubbles, chicle, abuelita, magic, bigger*, and many more—appear in color and in expressive fonts that are different from the text. Sentences swirl and swoop on many pages, just as Chavela flies through the air with her magic chicle. An appealing main character plus magic equals a beautiful story. An author's note expands on the facts about the sapodilla trees and the chicle harvested from them.

Burningham, John   4–8 YEARS
IT'S A SECRET!
Illustrated by John Burningham
Somerville, MA: Candlewick, 2009 | 978-0-7636-4275-4

A nighttime adventure with her pet answers Marie Elaine's question about where cats go after dark. The magic of word and picture makes Marie Elaine small as she and her cat escape out the cat door and navigate through the city to a party. Simple yet charming mixed-media illustrations become much more colorful in the party scenes. Whereas the background in the first half of the book is cream-colored or gray, the party pictures feature a textured black background and very colorful cats in fancy clothes. A couple of two-page spreads contain no text at all, with the preceding pages' words explained visually. Marie Elaine and her friend Norman, who has accompanied them, meet the Queen of the Cats, enjoy a good meal, dance, and finally go home. The last illustration, with a normal cat and normal-sized girl, may have readers wondering if it was all a dream. And that may be the beginning of a very interesting discussion.

Chaconas, Dori   4–8 YEARS
CORIANDER THE CONTRARY HEN
Illustrated by Marsha Gray Carrington
Minneapolis: Carolrhoda, 2007 | 978-1-57505-749-1 | library binding

An incorrigible chicken does the opposite of what she is supposed to do, frustrating Farmer and Mrs. Bucket and their daughter, Fanny. Everything comes to a head when Coriander sets up her nest in the middle of the road, blocking traffic and causing the Buckets to despair. Finally, Fanny, with a bit of reverse psychology, convinces her to move back to the henhouse. The illustrations, delightfully silly, show Coriander as a magazine-reading, skateboard-riding, popcorn-eating diva (check out her pink glasses); the other animals and humans come across just as funny. Coriander's replies to the Buckets' chiding are spelled out in large letters, as are the noises of the vehicles that are backed up on the road. A fun book for a lively read-aloud session.

Chen, Chih-Yuan   4–8 YEARS
GUJI GUJI
Illustrated by Chih-Yuan Chen
La Jolla, CA: Kane/Miller, 2004 | 978-1-929132-67-6

The familiar ugly duckling theme appears here, but it is remarkably fresh in this book first published in Taiwan. In this case, the odd egg that Mother Duck hatches produces a crocodile that blends right in with his siblings until three mean crocodiles accost him. Forced to decide where he belongs, Guji Guji stays with those who treat him as family, and the bad crocodiles meet a justified punishment. Charming artwork adds to the text, supplying a great dose of humor. The background color in many scenes reflects the mood: several pages featuring the crocodile trio are set in black or gray. Librarians and teachers will appreciate the nod to books; Mother Duck is oblivious to the new egg in her nest because she is reading, and later on she is shown reading to her four babies. This story would make a good source for discussions on adoption and what makes a family. For another take on crocodiles, fowl, and hatching unrelated eggs, see *Mrs. Chicken and the Hungry Crocodile* (Holt, 2003), by Won-Ldy Paye and Margaret H. Lippert.

Cronin, Doreen   3–7 YEARS
CLICK, CLACK, MOO: COWS THAT TYPE
Illustrated by Betsy Lewin
New York: Simon & Schuster, 2000 | 978-0-689-83213-0

Who knew that cows, armed with a manual typewriter, could type their demands for electric blankets? Farmer Brown finds that out, and when he balks at their request, he learns that these bossy bovines can also go on strike. When the chickens join the strike, Farmer Brown is forced to negotiate. Just when he thinks everyone is happy, the ducks get into the act. The incongruous images of cows using their hooves to type and animals demanding warm blankets provide the silly humor of this book. The comical illustrations, in watercolor, enhance the laugh-out-loud mood of the story. The sounds of the clicking, clacking typing, plus the typed notes, take shape in typewriter-type script. This book would make an excellent choice for reading aloud, with repetition of the main title throughout the book, the depiction of the angry farmer, and the antics of the disgruntled animals. Labor disputes and cows have never been so funny. Appealing absurdity, bovine-style, is also available in Margie Palatini's *Boo-Hoo Moo* (Harper-Collins, 2009) and Andy Cutbill's *The Cow That Laid an Egg* (HarperCollins, 2008).

Cronin, Doreen   4–8 YEARS
RESCUE BUNNIES
Illustrated by Scott Menchin
New York: Balzer + Bray/HarperCollins, 2010 | 978-0-06-112871-4

A group of veteran rescue bunnies (think first responders) is saddled with a trainee called Newbie. Rather clumsy but eager to help, Newbie accompanies the team on a mission to rescue a giraffe from a mudhole. Comical illustrations show the bunnies in their uniforms, doing their jobs and avoiding the nasty hyenas that threaten the giraffe. Adults reading this story to children will appreciate the additional comments and dialogue balloons, part of the illustrations, which incorporate lines from movies. These add a bit of irreverence to this sweet story with just enough of a humorous edge. This could be the only children's book to combine a spice rack, the Bunny Hop, and a nervous giraffe.

Curtis, Carolyn   3–8 YEARS
I TOOK THE MOON FOR A WALK
Illustrated by Alison Jay
Cambridge, MA: Barefoot, 2004 | 978-1-84148-611-6

With poetic language and stylized illustrations, this beautiful lullaby of a book invites the reader along on a walk through a young boy's town. An *aaab* rhyme scheme where the last line repeats the book's title creates a lulling rhythm and sense of cohesiveness. Jay's trademark paintings, rounded characters with skinny extremities, were created with alkyd oil paint on paper with a crackling varnish; close examination will reveal fine lines throughout, for a pleasantly classic effect. White space (off-white in this case) frames the illustrations, not with a defined line, but with a fuzzy border around each rectangle or half-circle, which enhances the duskiness of the time of day. Facts about the moon and nighttime conclude the book, making it an excellent source to combine literature and science.

Davies, Jacqueline   **4–8 YEARS**
THE HOUSE TAKES A VACATION
Illustrated by Lee White
Tarrytown, NY: Marshall Cavendish, 2007 | 978-0-7614-5331-4

An anthropomorphized house, determined to take a vacation when its family leaves, sets off on a trip. The travel, plus events at the seashore, takes a toll. The humor in this story comes from the clever wordplay of the text and the cartoon illustrations of oil and colored pencil. The expressions of eyes and mouths on the doors, windows, roof, and chimney help the reader or listener enter into the banter between these elements. Partying houseflies, little legs on the house, and animated inanimate objects make this a delightful romp. There's no place like home for a house to rest up from a holiday . . . and then the family returns.

Derby, Sally   **4–8 YEARS**
WHOOSH WENT THE WIND!
Illustrated by Vincent Nguyen
Tarrytown, NY: Marshall Cavendish, 2006 | 978-0-7614-5309-3

Being late to school can inspire some pretty good stories, but this one is a whopper. A little boy tells his teacher why the wind made him late, and she is *not* buying it. His imaginative stories, enhanced by color-saturated illustrations in acrylic paint and charcoal pencil, portray the situations in all their dandelion-, puppy-, and hat-blowing glory. (See figure 5.1.) Almost every page turn leads into the teacher's words in red, short and unbelieving, which in turn lead to more fanciful stories from the boy. A twist ending provides even more humor to this lively story. Another blustery book, *Flora's Very Windy Day* (Clarion, 2010) by Jeanne Birdsall, features a girl who rescues her little brother when they are blown away.

Figure 5.1 *Whoosh Went the Wind!*

Ellery, Amanda   **3–7 YEARS**
IF I HAD A DRAGON
Illustrated by Tom Ellery
New York: Simon & Schuster, 2006 | 978-1-4169-0924-8

When Mom orders Morton to play with his little brother, he imagines the toddler as something more interesting, including a dragon. Illustrations in charcoal, ink, and watercolor complement the text with bold imagination. The text itself is quite spare, with the illustrations telling the whole story, especially the limitations of a dragon playing basketball, swimming, or seeing a movie. The details such as the tiny shoes on the dragon's toes and the sunbathing dragon reading *DQ* magazine inspire hilarity. In the last scene, Morton, fed up with the dragon, plays with his little brother as a real boy and both have a great time. For an imaginative take on sibling issues, this book is hugely entertaining. Morton lets his imagination run wild again in *If I Were a Jungle Animal* (Simon & Schuster, 2009).

Fleming, Candace   **4–8 YEARS**
CLEVER JACK TAKES THE CAKE
Illustrated by G. Brian Karas
New York: Schwartz & Wade/Random House, 2010 | 978-0-375-84979-4

Poor Jack trades for or searches for the ingredients in his quest to make a beautiful cake, complete with walnuts and a strawberry. He intends to take the cake to the princess, celebrating her tenth birthday with a big party. But after meeting some hungry blackbirds, a wild troll, a dancing bear, and other obstacles, Jack arrives with nothing to present to the princess except this story of his journey from home to palace. Gouache-and-pencil illustrations present Jack as hardworking and determined, and the characters who thwart him as sometimes scary, sometimes comical. The endpapers frame the story with the delivery of the invitation to the party at the front and Jack regaling the princess with the story at the back. Notice the use of multiple illustrations on one page to suggest activity and the passage of time. Jack turns lemons into lemonade in this satisfying and clever tale.

Fletcher, Ralph   **3–8 YEARS**
THE SANDMAN
Illustrated by Richard Cowdrey
New York: Henry Holt, 2008 | 978-0-8050-7726-1

For those who have heard of the Sandman and his ability to help people fall asleep, but who have always wondered what he looks like, here he is revealed in all his tiny glory.

How does he produce the sand, which comes from dragons' scales? How does he travel around the world to sprinkle the sand in people's eyes? Read and find out! The droll illustrations combine large full-color art with some smaller brown-and-white drawings to move the action along. Children will want to linger at the illustrations of the Sandman's bedroom and workshop, where they will be able to identify all types of tiny items that he uses. Contrast the illustrations of the dragon, which are appropriately impressive and large, with the tiny Sandman and his mouse-drawn cart.

Foley, Greg   4–8 YEARS
WILLOUGHBY & THE MOON
Illustrated by Greg Foley
New York: Balzer + Bray/HarperCollins, 2010 | 978-0-06-154753-9

With unique illustrations in black, white, and silvery gray, this book enters the imagination of Willoughby Smith, who finds the moon on the other side of his closet door. A large snail accompanies him on his travels around the moon to help the snail find a ball. Adventures in a moon buggy and a space pod follow. Willoughby's room is black and white, but when he leaves it to step onto the moon, shiny silver becomes the dominant color. The contrast continues as Willoughby and the snail's body (but not its shell) appear as simply drawn black line figures, while all around them the art conveys depth and texture. One especially impressive spread is a map of the moon on one page, with a cutaway of the inner workings of the moon on the facing page. The text reads in a matter-of-fact manner, with Willoughby continually calming the rather fearful snail. This mirrors the text on the first page, where Willoughby's mother asks him if he is afraid. A reassuring yet adventuresome book, perfect for bedtime. Willoughby first shows up in *Willoughby & the Lion* (Bowen/HarperCollins, 2009), which combines black and white with gold.

Fox, Mem   5–8 YEARS
THE GOBLIN AND THE EMPTY CHAIR
Illustrated by Leo and Diane Dillon
New York: Beach Lane, 2009 | 978-1-4169-8585-3

The illustrations and text work together perfectly in this tale. A goblin, believing he is too ugly to be seen, becomes somewhat of a hermit. Interestingly, his entire face is never seen in the illustrations. But after many years he observes individual members of a farmer's family, all overcome with sorrow. At night and unseen, the goblin helps out with the fieldwork, gardening, and even comforting. The family members realize the aid this stranger has given and invite him in to eat. A strong sense of loss permeates the story. The deceptively spare and simple text and the illustrations of ink and watercolor express a gamut of emotions. Each page contains one square illustration with a border above, rendered in colored pencil and portraying the action that occurs immediately before the main illustration. The combination of Fox's storytelling and the Dillons' art make this tale of an ugly goblin beautiful.

Gay, Marie-Louise   4–8 YEARS
CARAMBA
Illustrated by Marie-Louise Gay
Toronto: Groundwood/House of Anansi, 2005 | 978-0-88899-667-1

This sweet and brave story begins with the assumption that cats can fly. But the title character cannot, and he feels badly about it. Soft illustrations of feats of cat derring-do and Caramba's attempts to master flying will bring a smile. With the help of his best friend, Portia the Pig, plus his cousins, Caramba finds wherein his talents lie—the water. The seascapes and landscapes, lovely in shades of green, provide details for the listener to explore and complement this gently humorous tale.

Graham, Bob   4–8 YEARS
APRIL AND ESME, TOOTH FAIRIES
Illustrated by Bob Graham
Somerville, MA: Candlewick, 2010 | 978-0-7636-4683-7

In this fanciful take on what happens to baby teeth that fall out, two small fairies convince their parents that they are old enough to collect a young boy's tooth and leave a coin. This tooth fairy family, portrayed as close and loving, invites young listeners behind the scenes as the parents give their approval and go over all the details of how to accomplish their mission. Ink-and-watercolor art shows two appealing little girls with wings, Dad with wings and a ponytail, Mom with wings and a tattoo, and their tiny cottage decorated with teeth, among other objects. The trip to Daniel's house and their work once they get there contains a few scenes of mild danger. (What about that owl? The tooth is in a cup of water! What if Daniel wakes up?) Ending scenes, on facing pages, present the tooth fairy parents putting their tired little ones to bed and the boy showing his coin to his grandma, providing closure on both ends of the story. With quiet energy, the text and illustrations provide a tale that is at once old-fashioned, but with touches of modern, as when the fairies receive calls on cell phones.

Heide, Florence Parry   4–8 YEARS
PRINCESS HYACINTH: THE SURPRISING TALE OF A GIRL WHO FLOATED
Illustrated by Lane Smith
New York: Schwartz & Wade, 2009 | 978-0-375-84501-7

As the title promises, unless she is strapped down or under a heavy crown or dressed in a gown with weights, the princess floats. She longs to get out from under her burden and, when the Balloon Man in the park lets her float with his balloons, she loves it. The illustrations will amuse young listeners. Who wouldn't like topiary animals, complicated systems to keep the princess grounded, and—always popular—underwear? The brush-and-ink characters, with oil-painted backgrounds, appear appropriately airy and weighty where they should. The words in the text even float up in the right places. The book ends with tea and popcorn; what could be better? Note the smallness of the princess in relation to the castle. This fantasy imbued with humor cinches that feeling of not always being in control of what happens.

Holt, Kimberly Willis   4–8 YEARS
SKINNY BROWN DOG
Illustrated by Donald Saaf
New York: Henry Holt, 2007 | 978-0-8050-7587-8

With its appealing animal illustrations and its feel-good storyline, this tale will delight just about anyone, especially those with a soft spot for lost dogs. Benny the Baker finds a dog on his doorstep. While Benny initially resists, the little dog wins him over by his popularity with customers and, ultimately, his life-saving deed. A variety of animals that act like humans populates this story. Even the dog, which usually acts like a canine, wears a suit coat and bowler hat and reads books. He does not talk, but the other characters do. With acrylic, gouache, watercolors, and colored pencils, Saaf has created a world where bears can be bakers and elephants can be regular customers. The variety of illustration sizes and placement provide visual interest and draw attention to the most heartwarming scenes. Endpapers feature a variety of bakery favorites that look good enough to eat!

Hurd, Thacher   3–8 YEARS
THE WEAVER
Illustrated by Elisa Kleven
New York: Farrar Straus Giroux, 2010 | 978-0-374-38254-4

A dreamy dance of a story, this book takes the view of the world from high above, where the weaver spins and dyes and works her threads into a beautiful tapestry that illustrates life on earth. The delicate and detailed illustrations fill the pages with happy scenes of families, animals, cityscapes, and elements of nature. The beginning features the rising sun and light-filled pages. As the story progresses and the day wears on, the illustrations begin to fill with a dusky blue. The weaver completes her work throughout the story, finally pulling her handiwork across the earth as people settle down to sleep and she rejoins her family for her own bedtime. These gorgeous illustrations present a soothing calm, matched by the poetic language of the text, which is filled with gentle rhythm and words of color and love. A note at the beginning explains a backstrap loom, the type portrayed in the illustrations.

Ichikawa, Satomi   3–7 YEARS
MY LITTLE TRAIN
Illustrated by Satomi Ichikawa
New York: Philomel/Penguin, 2010 | 978-0-399-25453-6

Beautiful watercolor artwork spreads over each page as a toy train makes its way with cars carrying stuffed animals. As they board, the animals announce where they want to go—the pond, the field, the forest, the mountains—and make animal noises. This provides opportunities for participation as listeners can chime in on the *quack-quacks* and the *baa-baas,* not to mention the *whoo-whoos* of the train. As the story rolls on, the train drops off each animal and continues on its way to Central Station. A wonderful blend of fantasy and reality, this story also shows how text and illustrations can contradict yet integrate. The pond where the duck stops is a fish bowl, the forest where the monkey disembarks is a large plant, and mountains are large pillows on the sofa; the illustrations provide the reality while the text names them as the animals do. A comforting journey story for young train lovers, this little train will take listeners to a satisfying conclusion and a happy reunion between two of the animals.

Johnson, Angela   5–9 YEARS
THE DAY RAY GOT AWAY
Illustrated by Luke LaMarca
New York: Simon & Schuster, 2010 | 978-0-689-87375-1

For those who wonder where those big parade balloons go when they are not floating tethered along the street, this story offers an imaginative tale of one balloon who made his plan to finally get away. Acrylic illustrations portray the balloon warehouse and the parade scenes all neatly enclosed in bordered squares and rectangles. As the story progresses, the ropes and balloons extend beyond these borders until, at the end, an unframed two-page spread shows Ray in his final escape. Interestingly, unlike the other balloon figures, Ray is never shown completely; bits of him are seen through windows or in the corner of an illustration. Even in that last picture, where he is whole, he appears as a black shadow in the twilit night. Young readers and listeners will enjoy the humorous illustrations and the balloon escape, while older readers may consider this a meditation on freedom.

Kneen, Maggie   3–8 YEARS
CHOCOLATE MOOSE
Illustrated by Maggie Kneen
New York: Dutton/Penguin, 2011 | 978-0-525-42202-0

Kneen has created a book for chocolate lovers. In this fanciful story, a moose takes a job at a bakery owned by Mrs. Mouse. Even as Moose does everything wrong and makes many messes in the kitchen, Mrs. Mouse, with her many children, finds something that he can do well. Beautifully textured illustrations give readers a moose and mice that look pettable. Cakes, sandwiches, and pancakes also have this touchable quality. Sound words such as *squish, slurp,* and *splat* are part of the text in just about every other page spread, where they appear in color and in a different font from the rest of the text. Readers and listeners will delight in the actions of the large but friendly Moose and the tiny mice. The word *chocolate* and illustrations of chocolate appear on many pages, even the endpapers. Yum!

Lehman, Barbara   5–8 YEARS
MUSEUM TRIP
Illustrated by Barbara Lehman
Boston: Houghton Mifflin, 2006 | 978-0-618-58125-2 | library binding

This wordless book follows a class on a field trip to an art museum, where one boy becomes separated from the group. As he wanders, he discovers a room with a display of small mazes in a glass case. Through the magic of fiction, he enters the mazes and solves them, running from one to the next. When he finally exits the mazes and room, he reunites with his class, and any question about whether his adventure actually happened is answered on the last page. With illustrations rendered in watercolor, gouache, and ink, Lehman delivers spare drawings of the human characters as colorful, with a bold black outline. The main character in a red sweatshirt stands out in each scene. Notice the perspective of space used: deep in some scenes, shallow in others. Adults who share this book with children may identify famous works of art that appear. Both adults and children will want to trace their way through the six mazes that the young boy solves. For another wordless adventure that involves a bit of magic, see Lehman's *Rainstorm* (Houghton Mifflin, 2007).

Litwin, Eric   3–8 YEARS
PETE THE CAT: I LOVE MY WHITE SHOES
Illustrated by James Dean
New York: HarperCollins, 2010, c2008 | 978-0-06-190622-0

Ideal for read-aloud, this story joins the title character as he walks down the street and gets into some messes. The shoes of which he is so proud turn colors, but that doesn't bother Pete, who keeps on walking and singing. The repetition in his song and the question asked after he steps into various things—not to mention identifying what he steps into—will make this a very participatory book for groups. The artwork beams with glorious color, especially in blue, red, and brown. And those white shoes, those ever-changing shoes, take center stage on the feet of Pete.

Lord, Cynthia   3–7 YEARS
HOT ROD HAMSTER
Illustrated by Derek Anderson
New York: Scholastic, 2010 | 978-0-545-03530-9

Young NASCAR fans will want to take this one out for a spin. Combining fast cars, charming animals, and humorous images, this story is a winner. Every other two-page spread features the hamster's friend, a large dog, asking him to make choices about size, color, and parts for his car. When Hamster is finally helmeted and ready to go, he faces larger competitors and bigger cars, but guess who wins? The acrylic illustrations, bright and colorful, feature mice mechanics and the inherent humor in animals putting together a race car. The front endpapers feature a race poster, while the back ones show the winner and his trophies. The questions about choice throughout will have young readers and listeners volunteering their own choices. Full of action, just like a race, this story doesn't stop until it reaches the finish line. For more driving fun, see Kristy Dempsey's *Mini Racer* (Bloomsbury, 2011), which features animals racing a variety of wheeled vehicles.

Mahy, Margaret   3–7 YEARS
BUBBLE TROUBLE
Illustrated by Polly Dunbar
New York: Clarion, 2008 | 978-0-547-07421-4 | library binding

The rhyming title gives just a sneak peek at what readers and listeners will find within: an exuberant story told in lilting rhyme and rhythm. A little girl blows a bubble, which somehow captures her baby brother. As he floats through the air, out of the window, and through the town, more and more people follow behind. These adults and children, who have first or last names that rhyme with each other or that contain similar internal sounds, make for quite an audience as the little guy floats higher and higher. With a well-aimed pebble in a slingshot and a catching quilt, several people save the baby. The watercolor-and-cut paper illustrations, full of jocularity and bright colors, mingle wonderfully with the humorous verse. The illustrations take up both pages in each page turn, with the baby usually in the far right corner, a dotted line showing his progress across the sky and page. First published in the United Kingdom, this story rolls along in a jolly blend of fantasy and fun.

Manushkin, Fran   **5–9 YEARS**
THE SHIVERS IN THE FRIDGE
Illustrated by Paul O. Zelinsky
New York: Dutton, 2006 | 978-0-525-46943-8

A family, living in a cold place, tries to keep warm and be brave, especially when a monster—a giant hand—comes in and removes items. The family finds itself surrounded by whipped cream towers, hills of oranges, and broccoli trees as they huddle in their little box. One by one, they go out to search for a warmer place to live. This book provides a wonderful example of the text relating the story on one level and the illustrations, comical and sly, completing that story. Each page abounds in humor, but some stand out for laugh-out-loud zaniness, including the scene where Mama jumps into what she thinks is a warm lake, but that eventually gels and has her stuck. All ends well as the family escapes the cold place, finds its rightful spot, and becomes once more warm and useful. The endpapers of the book, as well as the title, should give readers and listeners clues to what will happen, but the strength of the story and the illustrations can make those hearing it for the first time wonder what is really going on. Fantasy at its crazy, warmhearted best!

McDonald, Megan   **4–7 YEARS**
HEN HEARS GOSSIP
Illustrated by Joung Un Kim
New York: Greenwillow/HarperCollins, 2008 | 978-0-06-113876-8

Although young children may not have heard the word *gossip*, they will understand it after hearing this story. The barnyard animals pass along a secret from one to another, until it becomes clear that each one hears and tells it a little bit differently. Then it goes all the way back again until they find out the truth. The mixed-media illustrations, simple yet effective, include elements of collage and repetitive design almost like wallpaper on some pages. Of course, in every illustration, the animals' mouths are open, adding to the imagery of constant yakking. Teachers may want to play the telephone game, where children in a circle whisper a phrase from one to another, then see how much of it changes from the first person to the last. McDonald's story is a humorous introduction to a problem that can lead to hurt feelings. Pair with Marjorie Dennis Murray's *Hippo Goes Bananas!* (Marshall Cavendish, 2008) and *The Jungle Grapevine* by Alex Beard (Abrams, 2009).

McNaughton, Colin **5–8 YEARS**
CAPTAIN ABDUL'S LITTLE TREASURE
Illustrated by Colin McNaughton
Cambridge, MA: Candlewick, 2006 | 978-0-7636-3045-4

Avast, mateys! This pirate book starts out with a bang. Someone fires on Captain Abdul's pirate ship and leaves a treasure chest. When captain and crew discover a baby inside, left by Abdul's wife, Doris, they take to babysitting with all the verve that they put into pirating. The rowdy bunch dresses, feeds, entertains, and teaches the mini-pirate in a series of humorous scenes. The ink-and-watercolor illustrations, featuring humorously nasty-looking pirates, combine with a text full of piratespeak and pirate songs. Each page features a very large word or two at the beginning of the sentence, with numerous words and sentences in bold throughout. Adult readers can let their inner pirate out as they "Arrgh!" and "Yo-ho-ho!" their way through this hilarious yarn. Other humorous pirate stories include Laura Leuck's *I Love My Pirate Papa* (Harcourt, 2007) and Melinda Long's *Pirates Don't Change Diapers* (Harcourt, 2007).

McPhail, David **4–8 YEARS**
WATER BOY
Illustrated by David McPhail
New York: Abrams, 2007 | 978-0-8109-1784-2

When a young boy learns that humans are composed mostly of water, his imagination veers to extremes. Soon he refuses even to take a bath. With his mother's help, he overcomes his fear and from there, the story becomes a fantasy, with water from a faucet spelling his name and the force of his hand stopping waves. Eventually he learns to distill water and sunlight and finds a way to clean up rivers and oceans. This gentle book captures a child's fears, imaginings, and love of nature. The message that rivers need to be cleaned up is never overbearing, but integrates into the story of the boy's coming to understand the wider world. McPhail's soft illustrations appear in squares on most pages, but three scenes take the full two pages each, and these depict the boy in bigger settings: on beach cliffs, on the shore, and on a bridge overlooking the river. The endpapers, too, depict shore scenes that go off the edges of the page and feature the wildlife of the area. This book is smaller in size than the typical picture book, making it ideal for one-on-one reading and sharing.

Meschenmoser, Sebastian   **4–8 YEARS**

WAITING FOR WINTER

Illustrated by Sebastian Meschenmoser
Tulsa, OK: Kane Miller/EDC, 2009 | 978-1-935279-04-4

An imaginative look at the beginning of the cold season in a forest, this German import features animals who think, talk, and imagine. A squirrel, a hedgehog, and a bear find ways to take up time while waiting for snow to fall, including exercise and singing. Eventually, they search for this white, wet, cold, soft substance they have heard of and find some unusual substitutes. The illustrations of a fall of toothbrushes, socks, and tin cans come as humorous surprises. The text itself is not overly long, and many pages feature no words at all. Line drawings in muted black and white, with some brown and orange brushing the animals, reflect the bare winter season. The illustrations expand the text, which never mentions the odd items the animals find, and depict them realistically. When the real snow finally arrives, it is beautiful, and spread wordlessly over five full pages.

Monroe, Chris   **4–9 YEARS**

MONKEY WITH A TOOL BELT AND THE NOISY PROBLEM

Illustrated by Chris Monroe
Minneapolis: Carolrhoda, 2009 | 978-0-8225-9247-1 | library binding

For those who like their humor silly, yet detailed, this may be the perfect book. The title monkey, Chico Bon Bon, does indeed use a tool belt filled with both real and not-so-real tools. This busy little monkey fixes things around his house. As he searches for the source of a loud noise, he is pictured in various rooms in a detailed two-page spread. When he finally discovers the cause, it takes twelve panels of rectangular drawings to illustrate his plan to eliminate the noise. The brightly colored, humorous illustrations range from these large spreads to pages that have four or five small drawings. Chico takes precautions when he uses his tools, including donning a hard hat and earplugs, and he certainly demonstrates knowledge of all of the tools. The humor arises from the situations, which should provide lots of laughs. Chico makes his debut in *Monkey with a Tool Belt*. Pair with Marc Rosenthal's *Archie and the Pirates* (Harper Collins, 2009), which also offers goofy fun and detailed drawings.

Morales, Yuyi   **3–7 YEARS**

LITTLE NIGHT

Illustrated by Yuyi Morales
New York: Neal Porter/Roaring Brook, 2007 | 978-1-59643-088-4

Luxuriant illustrations that cover each two-page spread draw the reader and listener in, embracing them as Mother Sky does with her Little Night. Even though a fantasy, the characters and their actions resemble those of any mother and child who are preparing for bedtime, with a little one who hides. Little Night insists that her mother find her, and Mother Sky obliges. In keeping with the theme of approaching nighttime, the colors gleam in deep roses, blues, greens, and purples, finally studded with stars. The crocheted-cloud nightgown, Milky Way mustache, and planet hairpins provide beautiful touches. Reminiscent of *The Runaway Bunny* by Margaret Wise Brown, this story celebrates the love of mother and child, with a mother who will always care for her little one.

Muth, Jon J.   5–8 YEARS
ZEN SHORTS
Illustrated by Jon J. Muth
New York: Scholastic, 2005 | 978-0-439-33911-7

Can young children understand Zen? They can, in an elementary way, through this meditative book. Three children find a large bear named Stillwater in their backyard. Each of them spends time with the bear, who tells each child an old story from Buddhist and Tao roots, which is just what they need at the time. The watercolor-and-ink illustrations contain color in the main part of the story but become black and white on a light blue, green, or yellow background for the individual stories Stillwater tells. This device, the simple language, and the everyday situations (except for a large talking bear in the backyard!) go far to make Eastern philosophy understandable to young ones. From the illustrations only, one might be tempted to pronounce this book whimsical because it features a bear with a red parasol; that would cheapen it. Stillwater has a quiet elegance that fits perfectly with what he is trying to convey to the children. He appears again in *Zen Ties* (Scholastic, 2008), which introduces haiku, and *Zen Ghosts* (Scholastic, 2010), which features a Halloween setting.

Nakagawa, Chihiro   3–7 YEARS
WHO MADE THIS CAKE?
Illustrated by Junji Koyose
Honesdale, PA: Front Street, 2008 | 978-1-59078-595-9

Combine heavy machinery and birthday cake and out pops this delightful and detailed look at the construction of a dessert with construction equipment. Originally published in Japan, this book features a bevy of heavy trucks that mix the ingredients, pour the batter into the pan, and then bake it. After they frost and decorate the cake, it is presented to a little boy who, judging from his toys, loves construction machinery. From the illustration on the title page, it appears that the mother orders a cake from the construction workers. The text is spare—one line per page, just enough to tell what the machines are doing. Bright and mostly primary colors and the realistic-looking trucks will appeal to those who can't get enough of front loaders, backhoes, and dump trucks. Little people scramble all over the place, helping and signaling, and even taking a break, just like real construction workers. Look for one who has fallen in each scene. A wonderful blend of fantasy and reality.

O'Callahan, Jay **4–9 YEARS**

RASPBERRIES!

Illustrated by Will Moses
New York: Philomel/Penguin, 2009 | 978-0-399-25181-8

When Simon worked as a baker, before he was robbed and had to sell his shop, he would help a poor girl named Sally by providing bread for a penny. After more set-backs for Simon, Sally appears to him and gives him a pouch of dried raspberries. Much like Jack of beanstalk fame, Simon plants the seeds and wakes up to find rasp-berries growing on multiple bushes. When he cannot sell the fruit, he joins a baker in town in making raspberry tarts, which soon grow to be quite famous. Throughout the story, the taste of raspberries or of the tarts makes people exclaim or sing the word *raspberries,* which appears in red print and spreads across the page with extra letters. The liveliness of the text makes it a good read-aloud, while the folk art illustrations portray the people and setting in an old-time way. Reminiscent of the art of Grandma Moses, the illustrations are the work of her great-grandson. For a story of small-town life, with a touch of magic, *Raspberries!* is sweet indeed.

O'Malley, Kevin **5–10 YEARS**

CAPTAIN RAPTOR AND THE MOON MYSTERY

Illustrations by Patrick O'Brien
New York: Walker, 2005 | 978-0-8027-8935-8

With elements of Buck Rogers, *Star Trek,* and *Dinotopia,* plus action, suspense, and a little humor, this rip-roaring adventure practically bursts from its pages. Illustrated in panels, but with some large illustrations, the story contains elements of the graphic novel and the picture book. Some of the page turns feature a question that builds suspense before the reader discovers what happens on the next page. The twist in this fast-moving space opera: the main characters are dinosaurs, intelligent and outfit-ted in armor for their explorations. As they bounce from one seemingly inescapable situation to the next, they confront beasts with the help of their tools and their wits. Listeners and readers who enjoy science fiction, dinosaurs, and nonstop adventure will thrill to this story, which older teachers and parents will find reminiscent of books and movies of their childhood. Avid fans will also want to check out *Captain Raptor and the Space Pirates* (Walker, 2007).

Pelletier, Andrew T.   **4–8 YEARS**
THE TOY FARMER
Illustrated by Scott Nash
New York: Dutton, 2007 | 978-1-4287-4785-2

A little toy tractor with a farmer on board passes from father to son in this delightful story of unbounded imagination. Jed wakes up to find that the toy farmer has plowed his bedroom rug into a field in which a complicated plant quickly grows and bears a pumpkin. The plant and pumpkin exhibit a mechanical look in the brightly colored cartoon-style illustrations. As the plant grows, the farmer, tractor, and other toys all seem to be as big as Jed . . . or has he shrunk to their size? At this point, he convincingly enters into the farmer's world, as will the readers. The ending turns poignant as father and son share an understanding of this special experience. In the last few pages, the pumpkin morphs into the moon, still with its mechanical wind-up key.

Pinfold, Levi   **4–9 YEARS**
THE DJANGO
Illustrated by Levi Pinfold
Somerville, MA: Templar/Candlewick, 2010 | 978-0-7636-4788-9

A fascinating look at the life of a young Romany (Gypsy) boy, this book features an imaginary mischief maker. When a banjo breaks or when a horse is scared, Jean knows that the Django did it, even though he gets blamed. Watercolor illustrations combine full-page scenes and small scenes framed like old photographs. The detail, especially of faces, is rendered beautifully; the settings of the gypsy wagons, a town, and a gypsy camp provide the minutiae to make this cultural group come alive. Based loosely on Jean "Django" Reinhardt, a jazz musician, the story ends with information about him and his extraordinary talent. A story of family and the power of music to heal.

Polacco, Patricia   **4–8 YEARS**
GINGER AND PETUNIA
Illustrated by Patricia Polacco
New York: Philomel/Penguin, 2007 | 978-0-399-24539-8

Can a lady's pampered pig take her place when she must suddenly leave the country? With a little imagination enhanced by the outrageous illustrations, anything can happen! Ginger's pig, Petunia, inadvertently left alone, takes over everything she has seen Ginger do, including cooking, dressing in fancy clothes, teaching piano lessons, and attending parties. She still misses her long mud baths, though, which eventually lands her in a messy situation. But by that time Ginger arrives home and all is well. Brightly colored illustrations fill whole pages, except where the text resides, allowing the larger-than-life characters the space they need. With pencils and markers, Polacco renders a very believable, if fantastic, world. Ginger and Petunia come across as two grand and eccentric ladies. That one is a pig just doesn't matter. It adds to the fun.

Raschka, Chris   5+ YEARS
JOHN COLTRANE'S GIANT STEPS
Illustrated by Chris Raschka
New York: Richard Jackson/Atheneum, 2002 | 978-0-689-84598-7

This unique book fairly begs to be read with Coltrane's music playing in the background. Its story is about listening to the tempo, the instruments, the harmony, and the melody in the composition of the title. With watercolor-and-ink illustrations, abstract shapes of a box, snowflake, raindrops, and a sketch of a kitten come together and eventually go too fast and must be stopped. The author then explains what went wrong and begins again. The pages are numbered, unusual for a picture book, because the author refers to pages in his explanation. Raschka's jazz style demonstrates how music can be translated into picture and color and movement. Teachers and parents using this book with children may want to try other jazz compositions and have the children draw what they hear. For Raschka's take on a classical piece, see *Peter and the Wolf* (Richard Jackson/Atheneum, 2008). Complement this with *Jazz on a Saturday Night* (Blue Sky/Scholastic, 2007) by Leo and Diane Dillon or with Karen Ehrhardt's *This Jazz Man* (Harcourt, 2006).

Reed, Lynn Rowe   5–8 YEARS
OLIVER, THE SPACESHIP, AND ME
Illustrated by Lynn Rowe Reed
New York: Holiday House, 2009 | 978-0-8234-2193-0

When Carter discovers that his best friend, Oliver, invited another friend to go to the planetarium with him, he decides that he will build a spaceship and fly away without him. He comes up with a step-by-step plan to design and construct a spaceship with the help of an engineer, metalworker, welder, plumber, and electrician. Each adult helper's name is related to his or her work; for example, the plumber's name is Mr. Waters. The illustrations feature Reed's signature comic style, using acrylic paint, scanned and photographed objects, and Photoshop. The figures, childlike in style, contrast with some detailed plans of the actual spaceship and Carter's neatly printed to-do lists. Bold colors combine with photos of tools, pipes, and wire for a visually stimulating experience. With the text in first person, the story feels personal and immediate, as it explores the emotions of feeling left out and, at the end, doing the right thing.

129

Reynolds, Aaron

4–8 YEARS

BUFFALO WINGS

Illustrated by Paulette Bogan
New York: Bloomsbury, 2007 | 978-1-59990-062-9

Playing up the joke that recipes for buffalo wings contain no buffalo, this rollicking story follows a rooster who wants to prepare some food for the other animals while they watch a football game. In search of buffalo, he travels to a rodeo, national park, and water park, all of which have the word *buffalo* in their name, but with no luck. When he finally meets some buffalo, he discovers that the recipe calls for chicken wings. Bright watercolor illustrations cover each two-page spread and feature farm animals—and buffalo—in hilarious and human poses. With the popularity of cooking shows that attract all ages, this book will add some spice to storytimes with food or barnyard themes. It includes two recipes on the back endpapers. For more food fun, check out the author-illustrator team's first outing, *Chicks and Salsa* (Bloomsbury, 2005).

Rodriguez, Edel

4–9 YEARS

SERGIO SAVES THE GAME!

Illustrated by Edel Rodriguez
New York: Little, Brown, 2009 | 978-0-316-06617-4

A penguin who plays soccer wins the big game for his team. With a fairly simple color scheme of black and white, red and gold, and sometimes turquoise, the illustrations show Sergio's moves with gusto, both in his dreams (superbly!) and in reality (rather clumsily). Oil-based woodblock ink and digital media combine in these illustrations with fun touches; for example, check out Sergio's sleep mask. Although Sergio is selected last in any games, and his friends will choose even a fish before him, he knows that practice makes perfect and works hard in his role as goalie. In the end, he finds a unique way to win the championship. For sports lovers, those who are always chosen last, and those who like a fast-moving story, this book is a winner on all counts. For more penguin fun, see *Sergio Makes a Splash!* (2008).

Rumford, James

5–10 YEARS

NINE ANIMALS AND THE WELL

Illustrated by James Rumford
Boston: Houghton Mifflin, 2003 | 978-0-618-30915-3

A delightful combination of animals and numbers, this story takes place in India. On their way to a raja-king's party, nine animals reveal their gifts, each one bringing one more item than the animal before. Each successive animal throws out his or her gift, thinking it inferior after discovering what the next animal carries. The illustrations, described as "a collage of various Japanese papers decorated by the author and refined with brush, pen, and pencil," combine a delicacy of background with bold colors. Rumford creates appealing illustrations of the animals—both the partygoers and the animals that benefit from the discarded presents. The dimensions of the book, approximately eleven inches horizontal by eight inches vertical, work perfectly as the animals make their way from left to right to the palace. Near the end, the animals balance on top of each other, for which the book must be turned sideways. At the beginning and again at the end, notes about numbers and their origins elevate this already-impressive tale into a teachable moment about numerals.

Schachner, Judy   4–8 YEARS
SKIPPYJON JONES LOST IN SPICE
Illustrated by Judy Schachner
New York: Dutton, 2009 | 978-0-525-47965-9

The ever on-the-go Siamese kitten who thinks he is a Chihuahua has had several adventures since first appearing in 2003. In this one, familiar elements such as bouncing on his bed and traveling through his closet take Skippyjon into outer space, where he once again teams up with his Los Chimichangos, a pack of Chihuahuas who encourage him in his rhymes, Spanish words, and wacky adventures. With his can-do attitude, this little kitty is ready for anything, slowed down only by his ever-patient Mama Cat and teased by his three younger sisters. All of the illustrations, done in acrylics and pen and ink, feature a lot of *rojo* as befits a trip to the Red Planet, and green for the Martians. Many of the words of the text appear in different styles and sizes, especially the rhyming songs and the exclamations that Skippyjon loves to use. Great fun as a read-aloud, with ample opportunities for the reader to enter into the wonderful silliness that is Skippyjon Jones.

Schwarz, Viviane   4–8 YEARS
SHARK AND LOBSTER'S AMAZING UNDERSEA ADVENTURE
Illustrated by Viviane Schwarz and Joel Stewart
Cambridge, MA: Candlewick, 2006 | 978-1-4156-8140-4

The first thing readers and listeners will notice about this book is that it opens vertically rather than horizontally, enabling some illustrations to be quite tall. The premise that two friends, a lobster and a shark, discuss their fear of underwater tigers starts the story off with absurd humor. As they go to great lengths to build a fortress, they involve other sea creatures, including a fantastic deep-sea monster complete with human legs and butterfly wings. Dialogue balloons and some pages with panels give this book a graphic novel style. A good choice for read-alouds because of its size and unique perspective, this story will delight those who appreciate its weird humor. Check out the endpapers for more monstrous creatures of the deep.

Scotton, Rob   **3–8 YEARS**
RUSSELL THE SHEEP
Illustrated by Rob Scotton
New York: HarperCollins, 2005 | 978-0-06-059849-5

With his expressive face and humorous ideas, Russell the sheep makes sleeplessness fun. As the other members of his herd brush their teeth and hug their teddy bears, Russell faces a night of insomnia, trying all manner of remedies for catching some shut-eye. This book offers an excellent example of the illustrations telling more than the text, and usually in an extremely humorous way. Sheep sleeping with their legs straight up, Russell crammed into a car trunk, Russell's stocking cap bordering an illustration: guffaws are guaranteed. No one will nod off during this one. This woolly ruminant takes his unique ideas even further in *Russell and the Lost Treasure* (HarperCollins, 2006) and *Russell's Christmas Magic* (HarperCollins, 2007).

Selick, Henry   **4–8 YEARS**
MOONGIRL
Illustrated by Peter Chan and Courtney Booker
Cambridge, MA: Candlewick, 2006 | 978-0-7636-3068-3

In an out-of-this-world fantasy, a young boy attempting some moonlight fishing hooks a giant fish and is transported to the moon. There Leon meets the Moongirl, and together they stop the strange and sinister gargaloon from stealing the lightning bugs that are needed to relight the moon. The beautifully detailed illustrations, executed in pencil and digitally colored, shimmer with dark colors and shadowy backgrounds, just perfect for a moonlit night. Large faces with huge eyes (children's and pets') provide a pleasing up-close immediacy. (See figure 5.2.) If the whole look is reminiscent of recent animated movies, this reflects the author's and illustrators' backgrounds. Action sequences described in the text project this film feel, too. The imaginative story of how the moon gets its light and the appealing children and animal side characters make this story shine.

Figure 5.2   *Moongirl*

Shaw, Hannah   **4–8 YEARS**
SNEAKY WEASEL
Illustrated by Hannah Shaw
New York: Alfred A. Knopf, 2009 | 978-0-375-85625-9

The title character comes across as one guy that no one would want as a friend. Sneaky Weasel is mean, and full of himself on top of that. When no one comes to his party, he discovers that all the invitees loathe him, and he finds out what he must do to regain their trust and friendship. First published in Great Britain, this story assembles a collection of deliciously wacky illustrations both of the present-day Mr. Sneaky himself, in bright colors, and the remembered incidents of meanness in paler hues. Shaw uses pen and ink, printmaking techniques, and Photoshop to portray her animal characters which illustrate the oh-so-human characteristics, both good and bad, that make up this story of the importance of apologizing. Endpapers at the front feature Sneaky Weasel's ads for substandard or just plain mean products, and at the back, good and helpful products. Shaw's story is a wonderful selection for lessons in etiquette or for those who enjoy a story in which even the meanest can change to the nicest—almost!

Sierra, Judy   **4–8 YEARS**
TELL THE TRUTH, B.B. WOLF
Illustrated by J. Otto Seibold
New York: Alfred A. Knopf, 2010 | 978-0-375-85620-4

The Big Bad Wolf, invited to the library to tell the story of the Three Little Pigs, twists the truth so that he does not come off as the bad guy. But the listeners, other storybook and fairy tale characters, do not believe his explanation. With fun wordplay and funny digital illustrations, this story delights on a number of levels. Both children and adults will want to identify the various fictional characters, will enjoy B.B. Wolf's take on the traditional tale, and will be surprised at his solution to make amends for his lie. A couple of opportunities to sing in the story should make read-alouds even more fun. Big Bad Wolf also appeared in *Mind Your Manners, B.B. Wolf* (Knopf, 2007).

Spinner, Stephanie, reteller   **4–9 YEARS**
THE NUTCRACKER
Illustrated by Peter Malone
New York: Alfred A. Knopf, 2008 | 978-0-375-84464-5

The familiar story of *The Nutcracker*, known to many because of the ballet performed at Christmastime, appears in its magical glory here, with charming text and illustrations. The Christmas Eve scenes that take place in the home of Marie's family, including her dream of the Mouse King, show in the watercolor illustrations as burnished color appropriate to the night. Scenes depicting the Land of Sweets project brighter colors as the various dancers leap and twirl. Play the CD of Tchaikovsky's *The Nutcracker* that accompanies the book for the full visual-auditory experience. Another beautifully illustrated version is *The Nutcracker* by Susan Jeffers (HarperCollins, 2007). A humorous takeoff involving a video game is the musical-turned-picture book *A Nutty Nutcracker Christmas* (Chronicle, 2009) by Ralph Covert and G. Riley Mills.

Stead, Philip C.
A SICK DAY FOR AMOS McGEE
4–8 YEARS
Illustrated by Erin E. Stead
New York: Neal Porter/Roaring Brook, 2010 | 978-1-59643-402-8

Who knew that a sick day could be this much fun? Amos McGee, who works at the city zoo, always knows just what to do when he visits five of his favorite animals. But on a day when he stays home with a cold, the animals come to visit him. The woodblock print-and-pencil illustrations depict the world of Amos McGee in a limited palette, which draws attention to the main characters or objects on each page. Soft tans, blues, and greens predominate on most of the pages, with several spreads in Amos McGee's house seemingly bursting with color as yellow-striped walls fill the background. Bright red in a balloon, scarf, and socks provides a pleasing perkiness in some of the artwork. The text captures Amos's routine, his punctual ways, and his great love for the elephant, tortoise, penguin, rhinoceros, and owl. Pleasing repetition occurs when the animals at his house do the same things for him as he has always done for them. Despite some large animals, this is a calm and gentle story that won the Caldecott Medal in 2010.

Stevens, Janet, and Susan Stevens Crummel
HELP ME, MR. MUTT! EXPERT ANSWERS FOR DOGS WITH PEOPLE PROBLEMS
6+ YEARS
Illustrated by Janet Stevens
Orlando: Harcourt, 2008 | 978-0-15-204628-6

Dog lovers will howl with laughter and cat lovers will mew with delight at this humorous book, a collection of letters to canine counselor Mr. Mutt, supplemented by notes from The Queen, a cat who lives in the same house as Mr. Mutt. The questions revolve around typical dog problems: they want more food, they want their people to play with them, they do not want to be dressed in costumes, and they like to bark. Even the addresses on the letters reflect the canine theme. The hilarious text contains

Mr. Mutt's replies, complete with charts, graphs, and illustrations of what the advice seeker should do. Mixed-media artwork illustrates the kindly and wise Mr. Mutt and the imperious Queen, plus other dogs. Toward the end of the story, Mr. Mutt and The Queen have an altercation, which ladles on more visual humor, including ads in newspapers. The endpapers, too, contain newspaper ads that enhance the narrative. A must-read for animal lovers of all ages, this book could be used as a humorous read-aloud or even for teaching students how to write letters. Read Eileen Christelow's *Letters from a Desperate Dog* (Clarion, 2006) and *The Desperate Dog Writes Again* (Clarion, 2010) and Mark Teague's *Dear Mrs. LaRue: Letters from Obedience School* (Scholastic, 2002) for more fun with dogs and letters.

Stohner, Anu   **4–8 YEARS**
BRAVE CHARLOTTE AND THE WOLVES
Illustrated by Henrike Wilson
New York: Bloomsbury, 2009 | 978-1-59990-424-5

Charlotte the sheep saves her herd from torment by a gang of young sheep who like to pretend to be wolves. Her smarts and willingness to be different lead her to trick the gang. First published in Germany, this book combines a mildly suspenseful story with appealing illustrations, created with acrylics on cardboard. The texture of the sheep practically begs to be touched. For teachers or parents who want to reinforce the importance of not following the crowd, this story will also attract readers and listeners who enjoy a story about a clever main character. The title heroine first appears in *Brave Charlotte* (2005).

Wojciechowski, Susan   **4–9 YEARS**
A FINE ST. PATRICK'S DAY
Illustrated by Tom Curry
New York: Random House, 2004 | 978-0-385-73640-4 | paper

Set in Ireland, this magical and satisfying story concerns two towns that compete annually for the best-decorated place for St. Patrick's Day. When the people of one town help a leprechaun whose cows are in trouble, they know they will not be able to finish their decoration, but they find they have been rewarded anyway. Folk art illustrations of wondrous texture capture the villages, their inhabitants, and the work they are about. Rich colors saturate the pages with a mix of two-page spreads, one-and-a-half-page spreads and one page, with most of the text in white space. A fine book for read-alouds, and not just for St. Patrick's Day.

Wojtowicz, Jen   **4–8 YEARS**
THE BOY WHO GREW FLOWERS
Illustrated by Steve Adams
Cambridge, MA: Barefoot Books, 2005 | 978-1-84148-686-4

Strange, yet familiar. Odd, yet not disturbing. Somehow the fact that flowers grow out of the body of Rink Bowagon at the time of the full moon seems normal because his whole family skews exotic. While the children at school shun him, he forms a connection with the new girl, Angelina, who has one leg shorter than the other. With the help of a shoe that he designs and makes for her, they attend a dance, and he finds out a secret about that flower that always appears behind her ear. A fantasy, this tale is also a school story, with normal petty jealousies and teasing. Look for the unusual names of the students. The acrylic illustrations, especially the flowers, bring loveliness to each page. The two main characters, expressed as serene and happy in text and art, project an appealing sweetness in their differentness. Small illustrations of scissors, a boy at a desk, a needle and thread, and much more decorate the pages of text facing one-page illustrations. As the connection between Rink and Angelina blossoms, the ending is not surprising, but is instead a satisfying answer to "And then what happened?"

Yaccarino, Dan   **4–8 YEARS**
LAWN TO LAWN
Illustrated by Dan Yaccarino
New York: Alfred A. Knopf/Random House, 2010 | 978-0-375-85574-0

Lawn ornaments—some people love them, while others would describe them as tacky or creepy. But in this story, lovable (and almost human) wins out. A gnome, deer, flamingo, and jockey, named Norm, Betty, Flo, and Jack, respectively, face disposal in the trash truck if they cannot follow their beloved friend Pearl when she moves to a new house. As they make their journey, they meet other lawn ornaments, gargoyles, and statues, all the while avoiding the garbage trucks. Just when they arrive within sight of Pearl's house, lion statues thwart their plan to enter through the gate. But what was once an enemy becomes a friend, and they are delivered by truck to their joyous reunion with Pearl. Humorous gouache illustrations take the ornaments on the road, where statues come alive in bold color. The highly colorful endpapers, too, feature weathervanes, a mailbox, a totem pole, a carousel horse, fountains, and other statues as appealing figures that the characters may have met on their way. Snappy dialogue ensures that each ornament demonstrates a distinct personality in this fun story.

Yolen, Jane **5–9 YEARS**
COME TO THE FAIRIES' BALL
Illustrated by Gary Lippincott
Honesdale, PA: Wordsong/Boyds Mills, 2009 | 978-1-59078-464-8

The prolific Yolen offers another book in the realm of fantasy, this one a delight to ear and eye. The rhyming text tells of the ball being planned and the preparations of the fairies that want to attend. For extra drama, a Cinderella-type character emerges who owns only a torn dress. Eventually they all arrive at the ball, including the fairy who comes in late but with a beautiful dress, and who attracts the attention of the prince. The exquisite watercolor illustrations show fairies at all stages of preparation, with such fun details as a "Mom" tattoo, thick glasses, and striped stockings. Their transportation to the ball includes wonderfully imaginative uses of rabbits, turtles, and frogs, as well as other woodland animals. Dominant colors of green, gold, orange, and tan reflect the natural habitat of the fairy folk. The rhymed text conveys the hurry and hoopla of getting ready, the music and dancing of the ball, and a love story at the end. The first and last pages feature scrolls with stylized lettering that announce the ball and the wedding, respectively. For those who love fantastic worlds, especially those of fairies and princesses, this book will enchant.

Ziefert, Harriet **4–8 YEARS**
BY THE LIGHT OF THE HARVEST MOON
Illustrated by Mark Jones
Maplewood, NJ: Blue Apple, 2009 | 978-1-934706-69-5

The orange, gold, and red of autumn permeate this book, a blend of reality and fantasy. What begins as day's end is magically transformed, with a gust of wind, into a party of leaf people. Pastel illustrations bring texture and color to pictures that spread to the edge of pages, with text surrounded by the artwork. Leaf children and leaf adults sport pumpkin heads and leafy trunks and extremities, with clothes, hats, and footwear just like humans. Their activities, too, mimic those of humans: bobbing for apples, stacking pumpkins, and eating pie. Ideal for a lesson on autumn, this visually stunning book will appeal at any time of year to those who love the colors, smells, and sounds of fall. Celebrate other seasons with Ziefert's *Snow Party* (2008) and *Butterfly Birthday* (2010). Pair this with Nancy Raines Day's Halloween-themed *On a Windy Night* (Abrams, 2010) and compare mood.

Folktales and Fairy Tales

The picture books in this section represent stories that have arisen from the oral and literary traditions of many cultures and countries, including folktales, fairy tales, tall tales, traditional tales, legends, myths, fables, and trickster tales. From classic favorites to new discoveries, these books teach and entertain as they have through the ages.

Aesop   **4–9 YEARS**
THE CONTEST BETWEEN THE SUN AND THE WIND
Retold by Heather Forest
Illustrated by Susan Gaber
Atlanta: August House LittleFolk, 2008 | 978-0-87483-832-9

When the wind brags of his strength, the sun challenges him to see who can take off the coat of a man. The wind tries with his mightiest blowing and howling, but the man just clutches his coat more tightly. Then the sun, with heat and light, causes the man to remove the coat on his own. Dark colors, especially gray for the wind, and bright yellow for the sun, aptly illustrate this struggle between force and gentleness. The facial expressions of the wind and the sun indicate this mean-friendly dichotomy, too. The illustrations include scalloped-edged borders, full spreads, quarter-pages, and several pages to be turned sideways. This variety moves the story along, just like the man who walks on the road toward rainbows of light.

Alley, Zoë B.   **4—8 YEARS**
THERE'S A WOLF AT THE DOOR: FIVE CLASSIC TALES
Illustrated by R. W. Alley
New York: Neal Porter/Roaring Brook, 2008 | 978-1-59643-275-8

With its large size and graphic novel style, this book provides a perfect vehicle for the title character, whose inflated sense of his power stands out in these episodic adventures. Although most of the stories included here will be familiar—The Three Little Pigs, The Boy Who Cried Wolf, Little Red Riding Hood, and The Wolf in Sheep's Clothing—the continuation from one to the next pulls the whole narrative together, ending with The Wolf and the Seven Little Goslings, wherein the embattled wolf finally gives up. A sly sense of humor permeates the text and illustrations, with the fashion-obsessed Little Red Riding Hood and the comments of the sheep in The Boy Who Cried Wolf just a few of the highlights. Adults as well as children will appreciate the mix of the familiar and new, delivered in a fun comic style.

Arnold, Caroline   **4—8 YEARS**
THE TERRIBLE HODAG AND THE ANIMAL CATCHERS
Illustrated by John Sandford
Honesdale, PA: Boyds Mills, 2006 | 978-1-59078-166-1

Set in the north woods of Wisconsin, this story of lumberjacks and the creature they befriend is enhanced by woodcut illustrations that capture the larger-than-life characters. The typeface and illustrations lend an old-time style to this story which, though original, is based on the century-old stories of the hodag and the lumberjack Olee Swensen. In this version, three animal catchers want to capture the hodag for a zoo. Although a fearsome beast in appearance, the hodag is a friend of the lumberjacks, who outwit the animal catchers to protect him. Many of the black-and-white illustrations are enclosed in borders and take up the whole page opposite that of the text. In some of these bordered boxes, the illustration escapes outside of the border, especially in those depicting the hodag—he is just too big! Several two-page spreads feature unbordered illustrations, including a marvelous confrontation scene between burly lumberjacks and mousy animal catchers. Adults and children alike will cheer for the lumberjacks and the friendly hodag as they outsmart the bad guys.

Aylesworth, Jim, reteller   4–8 YEARS
THE MITTEN
Illustrated by Barbara McClintock
New York: Scholastic, 2009 | 978-0-439-92544-0

In this retelling of a classic tale, the mitten belongs to a little boy. When he loses one of the mittens made by his loving grandmother, its inviting warmth attracts a squirrel, a rabbit, a fox, and a bear. Improbably, they all squeeze in and achieve the warm coziness they seek. But when a mouse tries to wedge in, disaster results. McClintock's lovely illustrations display an antique charm, especially of the boy and his grandmother. Immersing oneself in the text and illustrations is like wrapping oneself in a warm fuzzy blanket. Interesting examples of framing abound in these illustrations, with literal frames around the pictures in the first few pages and then a combination of open and framed illustrations as the story progresses. The size of the illustrations also varies, with larger pictures as more animals push their way into the mitten. A gentle tale, especially for younger listeners, who will be attracted by the repetition as each animal tries to talk its way into the mitten, and the anticipation for what will surely happen when too many squeeze in. Extra bonus: a recipe for hot cocoa on the back cover. Similar, but using a different setting and set of animals, is Mary Casanova's *One-Dog Canoe*, set in the north woods.

Brett, Jan   4–8 YEARS
THE THREE SNOW BEARS
Illustrated by Jan Brett
New York: G.P. Putnam's Sons, 2007 | 978-0-399-24792-7

Brrr! Brett's realistic illustrations, rendered in watercolor and gouache, will make readers and listeners practically feel the cold in this Arctic rendition of Goldilocks and the Three Bears. Aloo-ki, searching for her sled dogs, wanders into the bears' igloo. Instead of porridge, chairs, and beds, the little girl samples soup, boots, and fur bed covers. In the meantime, the bear family finds her dogs, a side story told in smaller illustrations that serve as borders on each two-page spread. In a clever presentation, Arctic animals hold these circular illustrations. (See figure 6.1.) With realistic costumes, Aloo-ki and the bears bring a traditional Inuit look to the familiar tale. Look for special touches, such as the penguin totem outside the bears' igloo, the storage of clothes in a hanging basket, and the animal-shaped soup bowl. A great selection for teachers seeking multicultural retellings of familiar stories. For a traditional take on this tale, see *Goldilocks and the Three Bears* (Scholastic, 2003) by Jim Aylesworth. A Renaissance-themed *Goldilocks and the Three Bears* (Marshall Cavendish, 2009) is retold and illustrated by Gennady Spirin. Anthony Browne's *Me and You* (Farrar Straus Giroux, 2010) offers a modern urban version.

Figure 6.1 *The Three Snow Bears*

Bruchac, Joseph, and James Bruchac, retellers   **4–8 YEARS**
RACCOON'S LAST RACE
Illustrated by Jose Aruego and Ariane Dewey
New York: Dial/Penguin, 2004 | 978-0-8037-2977-3

Because of his long legs and lean body, Azban the Raccoon beats every animal in races. But wait! Don't raccoons have short legs and plump bodies? This *pourquoi* tale, which seeks to answer a why question, explains how raccoons came to be their present shape. From the oral tradition of the Abenaki, versions of the Azban tales can be found in other American Indian nations, according to the author's note at the beginning of this book. The text, perfect for storytelling, is enhanced by illustrations rendered in pen and ink, gouache, and pastel. The colors of nature in the first part of the book—green, brown, and autumn orange—contrast with the grays, deep blues, and black of the mountain where Azban meets his fate. Be sure to read other books by the father-son Bruchac team, also illustrated by Aruego and Dewey, such as *Turtle's Race with Beaver* (Dial, 2003) and *How Chipmunk Got His Stripes* (Dial, 2001).

Deedy, Carmen Agra, reteller   **4–8 YEARS**

MARTINA THE BEAUTIFUL COCKROACH: A CUBAN FOLKTALE

Illustrated by Michael Austin
Atlanta: Peachtree, 2007 | 978-1-56145-399-3

Forget all preconceived notions of cockroaches; Martina Josefina Catalina Cucaracha is beautiful. As she receives suitors in her family home in a street lamp, she follows her grandmother's advice about how to sort out the good from the bad. In the end, as in all good tales, she finds true love—with the little mouse whose weak eyes cannot see her beauty. The acrylic illustrations, bold in their color and size, display a sly humor, as does the text. Readers and listeners will cheer as Martina rejects a vain rooster, a smelly and selfish pig, and a sneaky lizard. On subsequent readings, they may want to see if they can spot the clever mouse in early scenes. A sweet ending tops off this tale.

DeFelice, Cynthia   **4–8 YEARS**

ONE POTATO, TWO POTATO

Illustrated by Andrea U'Ren
New York: Farrar Straus Giroux, 2006 | 978-0-374-35640-8

Mr. and Mrs. O'Grady, though very poor, are satisfied with what they have. When Mr. O'Grady finds a magic pot that doubles whatever is placed in it, they use it wisely. After an unfortunate fall, in which two Mrs. O'Gradys come out, Mr. O'Grady hops in, too, and soon there are two couples. But since each one wanted a best friend, this works perfectly for them. The pen-and-gouache illustrations perfectly capture the poor characters and the sparse living conditions—the O'Gradys are both drawn unbelievably thin—and then the duplicated potatoes and coins and candles. A timeless quality imbues this tale, which delights with its humor and magic.

Demi   **6+ YEARS**

THE HUNGRY COAT: A TALE FROM TURKEY

Illustrated by Demi
New York: Margaret K. McElderry/Simon & Schuster, 2004 | 978-0-689-84680-9

With her distinctive paint-and-ink artwork and excellent storytelling, Demi presents the story of wise man Nasrettin Hoca. Because he likes to help people, he finds himself dirty and smelling of goat just before a friend's banquet. When he is rejected because of his appearance, he finds a clever way to make a point about friendship and hospitality. Based on stories about the real Nasrettin Hoca, a Turkish philosopher, teacher, and humorist, this tale brings out his common sense and sense of humor. The illustrations, bordered in a Middle Eastern design and filled with people, delight the eye with bold colors, cultural integrity, and that humor with which Nasrettin taught his lessons. This sumptuous book would be a good introduction to Middle Eastern folktales or discussions of judging by appearances. For another Nasrettin tale, see Eric A. Kimmel's *Joha Makes a Wish* (Marshall Cavendish, 2010).

Fleischman, Paul   **4–10 YEARS**
GLASS SLIPPER, GOLD SANDAL: A WORLDWIDE CINDERELLA
Illustrated by Julie Paschkis
New York: Henry Holt, 2007 | 978-0-8050-7953-1

A beautiful rendering of Cinderella stories from a variety of countries, this book delivers a pleasing story and an appreciation of cultural differences. Just as the title refers to the different styles of footwear for Cinderella, other differences pop up in how she came to wear a beautiful dress and how she was helped when she was hungry. The folk art style, rendered in gouache, is a perfect match for this version of the tale. Each page or section includes a label with the name of the country from which that element of the story comes. Traditional symbols of the country in two-tone color surround bordered squares or rectangles of art and bordered text; these complement but do not distract from the main illustration. Endpapers consist of a world map with labeled countries that inspired the story. This collection of Cinderella tales testifies to their far-reaching appeal and origins.

Griffin, Kitty   **4–8 YEARS**
THE RIDE: THE LEGEND OF BETSY DOWDY
Illustrated by Marjorie Priceman
New York: Atheneum/Simon & Schuster, 2010 | 978-1-4169-2816-4

Set in American colonial times, this story introduces young Betsy, who wants to help the colonists fight King George. Although she knows she cannot be a soldier, her skills as a horsewoman come in handy as she rides to warn General Skinner about the approaching British Army. The emotionally and physically difficult journey receives fine treatment in the exciting text and active illustrations. Rendered in gouache and ink, the artwork features bold line and color, with much of it in dark purples, blues, and black during her nighttime ride. Was there a real Betsy Dowdy? No one knows, but her story is legend, as explained in an author's note at the end. Don't miss the endpapers, which depict a map delineating the route Betsy took from her home to General Skinner's camp.

Grimm, Jacob and Wilhelm   **6–9 YEARS**
HANSEL AND GRETEL
Retold by Rachel Isadora
Illustrated by Rachel Isadora
New York: G.P. Putnam's Sons, 2009 | 978-0-399-25028-6

In this version of the familiar tale, Africa becomes the setting, reflecting Isadora's ten-year residency there. The oil paint, printed paper, and palette paper illustrations burst with color and texture in their portrayal of clothing, houses, and natural elements. Readers will enjoy searching for African animals in many of the scenes. As befits the tale, the stepmother is sufficiently mean, the witch is very wicked, and the children are beautiful and resourceful. The illustrations cover each two-page spread and even appear to go beyond the edges of the page, affirming the vastness of each scene of the jungle or the night. Note the details in this visual feast, such as the witch's torn-paper hair, the edges of which are rendered a matted, sickly-white color, or the blue and white clouds floating in the sky of pure white. See Isadora's other fairy tales with African influence, including *The Ugly Duckling* (2009), *Rapunzel* (2008), *The Fisherman and His Wife* (2008), *The Twelve Dancing Princesses* (2007), and *The Princess and the Pea* (2007). For another variant of this tale, read Cynthia Rylant's *Hansel and Gretel* (Hyperion/Disney, 2008).

Hamilton, Martha, and Mitch Weiss   **4–9 YEARS**
THE GHOST CATCHER:
A BENGALI FOLKTALE
Illustrated by Kristen Balouch
Atlanta: August House LittleFolk, 2008 | 978-0-87483-835-0

Although ghosts do inhabit this story, readers should not expect scary specters; rather, the ghosts reveal themselves as silly creatures easily fooled by a young man. He is a barber, a soft touch for a hard-luck story, but, under orders from his wife to increase their income, he finds a way to make money by fooling two ghosts with a mirror. Soon he has tricked them into bringing him money, building sheds, and filling them with rice. The bright, uncluttered illustrations, colorful and smooth on a textured background, depict the clothes and buildings of India. (See figure 6.2.) Although uncomplicated, the illustrations reveal the characters in all their emotions and reactions. The endpapers contain miniature portraits of the main characters and others who appear in minor roles. An author's note at the end provides information about barbers in India, tales in Bengal, and the original texts of this folktale.

Figure 6.2   *The Ghost Catcher*

Hawes, Louise   4–10 YEARS
MUTI'S NECKLACE:
THE OLDEST STORY IN THE WORLD
Illustrated by Rebecca Guay
Boston: Houghton Mifflin, 2006 | 978-0-618-53583-5

With the gift of a necklace from her father, a young girl grows up in ancient Egypt secure in the love of family. She goes to work for the Pharaoh and loses the necklace in the river, then defies Pharaoh until the court magician can retrieve the necklace. Based on an old tale that concentrated much more on the magician's role, this retelling bestows a name and backstory on the girl. Sumptuous full-page illustrations in watercolor and acryla gouache capture the beauty of Muti, the grandeur of the Pharaoh, and the majesty of the river scenes. Facing pages containing text are set on a lightly colored, textured background that resembles papyrus. The family scenes make this story relatable to twenty-first century children; the setting and elements of magic give it a sense of otherness essential to the tale.

Heller, Janet Ruth   4–8 YEARS
HOW THE MOON REGAINED HER SHAPE
Illustrated by Ben Hodson
Mt. Pleasant, SC: Sylvan Dell, 2006 | 978-0-9764943-4-8

The moon, personified by a Native American woman, changes from large to small when confronted by the sun. Guided by a comet embodied by a warrior, Moon travels to the home of a woman who shows her how people and animals rely on the moon. Rendered in acrylic paints, handmade papers, wallpaper, pencil crayons, gesso, ink, and glue, the stunning illustrations feature stylized landscapes and skyscapes. Each page contains a border design with the moon in the upper and lower corner in a different phase, so that flipping through the book quickly shows the moon go from full to waning to waxing to full once more. End material includes facts and projects related to the moon, including Native American names for the full moon by month. Heller's book is ideal for teachers covering Native American themes or even science. It is a good example of a *pourquoi* tale.

Hodges, Margaret, reteller   4–8 YEARS
DICK WHITTINGTON AND HIS CAT
Illustrated by Mélisande Potter
New York: Holiday House, 2006 | 978-0-8234-1987-6

The old story of Dick, who goes from poor boy to lord mayor of London, receives a vigorous retelling. The text is replete with folktale conventions, including stylized

147

Figure 6.3   *Dick Whittington and His Cat*

language, good and evil characters, a recurring motif (bells), and a happy ending, making it perfect for storytelling. The illustrations of inks and gouache combine fine lines and muted colors to portray old London, a medieval house, and the sea, with several scenes of the Barbary Coast and royal palace in richer reds, blues, and greens. (See figure 6.3.) All will cheer for Dick as he overcomes his past, becomes a rich man, and uses his wealth to help others. The book concludes with an author's note about Dick Whittington, chapbooks, and the bells of London.

Hopkins, Jackie Mims   **4–8 YEARS**
THE GOLD MINER'S DAUGHTER: A MELODRAMATIC FAIRY TALE
Illustrated by Jon Goodell
Atlanta: Peachtree, 2006 | 978-1-56145-362-7

From the cover and first few pages, the reader enters the story as if walking into a theater and joining animal characters who sit watching the screen. The show begins in muted black and white but then quickly turns to color. Oil illustrations depict the daughter, her father, the villain, and various fairy tale characters, all after gold. Gracie plays the strong title character who defends her father and her honor and who eventually comes across a bigger treasure appropriate to the western setting—oil. Specifically designed for reading aloud, the book includes symbols throughout the story for audience participation. The framing device of setting the movie within a theater allows listeners to feel as if they are in the story. The inclusion of familiar characters such as Goldilocks, the Three Pigs, and Rapunzel adds a clever touch.

Isaacs, Anne   **4–9 YEARS**
DUST DEVIL
Illustrated by Paul O. Zelinsky
New York: Schwartz & Wade, 2010 | 978-0-375-86722-4

For a tall tale with enough vibrant energy to fill the whole state of Montana, this story about Angelica Longrider, a.k.a. Swamp Angel, takes readers to that western state in the 1830s. Combining the outsized deeds of a giant woman, much like the Paul Bunyan tales, with the western adventure of Backward Bart and his band of desperadoes, this tale swaggers with exaggeration and humor. The illustrations—oils painted on wood veneers—are bordered as rectangles or ovals, letting much of the wood show in the margins and lending a rustic look to this story, much of which takes place in the wide-open spaces of the West. Backward Bart and his gang provide lots of comic action, while Angel shines through as the heroine, along with her horse. And how she found her horse—that's a rip-roaring episode in this exuberant tale! Isaacs and Zelinsky collaborated on the original *Swamp Angel* (Dutton, 1994).

Javaherbin, Mina   **4–10 YEARS**
THE SECRET MESSAGE
Illustrated by Bruce Whatley
New York: Hyperion/Disney, 2010 | 978-1-4231-1044-6

Inspired by a poem by Rumi (Persian, thirteenth century), Javaherbin and Whatley create the world of a Persian merchant and his family. In his shop he keeps a parrot from India. Bright colors infuse the large illustrations, which on most page spreads take up one and a half pages. Text on the side, framed by a thin black line, focuses attention on the large illustration and the fabrics, foods, containers, and birds therein. When the merchant prepares for a trip to India, he asks everyone in his household, including his parrot, what they would like. The parrot asks only that the story of his life in a cage be told to his family in India. The merchant is shocked by the birds' reactions; he receives a second shock when he comes back to Persia and tells his parrot what happened. The illustrations reinforce the atmosphere of sumptuous luxury of the merchant and his family, while bringing home the message of freedom.

Kajikawa, Kimiko   **4–10 YEARS**
TSUNAMI!
Illustrated by Ed Young
New York: Philomel, 2009 | 978-0-399-25006-4

An old tale takes on new life in this story of Ojiisan, a wise old man who senses a change and soon knows that something beyond an earthquake is coming. He makes a supreme sacrifice—burning his extensive rice fields—in order to save the villagers who are on the beach. By the time the tsunami strikes, the people have come running to help save the fields and so are spared. The illustrations of gouache, pastel, and collage take center stage, as they occupy nearly ten inches of each vertical page spread, with the text in less than two inches at the bottom. Identifying the materials used in various scenes, such as woven baskets, straw, and tissue paper, could be used as an introduction to an art lesson for all ages and grade levels. Contrasts and textures—the flat blue sea versus the rough gray mountains—enhance the visual experience. Taking on huge concepts such as the power of nature and the destruction of fire and water, artist and author together have created a large and awesome story.

Karas, G. Brian   **4–8 YEARS**
YOUNG ZEUS
Illustrated by G. Brian Karas
New York: Scholastic, 2010 | 978-0-439-72806-5

How can ancient Greek myths be told in a way that appeals to young children? *Young Zeus* accomplishes this, with an energetic story that imagines the childhood of the Greek god. As told by Amaltheia, an enchanted goat, the story begins with Zeus as a baby and follows him through his boyhood on Crete. As soon as his plan to rescue his brothers and sisters succeeds, arguments ensue over who will be the boss. All this is faithful to the original story, told with suspense and emotion, helped greatly by the gouache-and-pencil illustrations, which contain touches of humor. Note the size of Zeus in many illustrations, especially those that show him with his father and mother and with the netherworld creatures, where he appears as very small. Young listeners will revel in the energy and action of the illustrations, full of battles and monsters, impossible deeds and fantastic characters. Karas vividly portrays the supreme Greek god plus a supreme case of sibling rivalry.

Kellogg, Steven
THE PIED PIPER'S MAGIC

Illustrated by Steven Kellogg
New York: Dial, 2009 | 978-0-8037-2818-9

4–8 YEARS

With Steven Kellogg's wonderfully detailed illustrations, this story offers a retelling of the Pied Piper tale and how he rids a city of rats. The twists: parents who are forced by the evil grand duke to work in a factory and the magic of backwards words, which bring love and peace to the city. The gorgeous artwork will encourage young listeners to study the pictures, rendered in ink, pencil, watercolor, and acrylic. Even scenes depicting crowds of children and parents feature distinctive faces and bodies. Magic music issuing from the piper's pipe comes out colorfully, full of flowers and butterflies and words. The book has a happy ending for everyone, including the grand duke, who falls in love. For a very different slant to the Pied Piper story, see Colin Bootman's *The Steel Pan Man of Harlem*.

Kimmel, Eric A.
CACTUS SOUP

Illustrated by Phil Huling
Tarrytown, NY: Marshall Cavendish, 2004 | 978-0-7614-5155-6

5–9 YEARS

Taking the old tale of Stone Soup to Mexico and the time of the revolution, this story follows the familiar plot, but substitutes a cactus thorn for the stone. Watercolor-and-ink illustrations, rich in tans, oranges, and pale greens, are large and filling (much like the soup), taking over whole pages and sometimes two-page spreads. In keeping with the setting, Spanish words, especially for food items, appear in italics throughout the text. A glossary of these words concludes the book. An author's note provides a short explanation of the Mexican Revolution and drawings of Pancho Villa and Emiliano Zapata. Compare with other variations, such as *Stone Soup* by Jon J. Muth (Scholastic, 2003), set in China, and *Kallaloo! A Caribbean Tale* by David and Phillis Gershator (Marshall Cavendish, 2005).

Kimmelman, Leslie
THE LITTLE RED HEN AND THE PASSOVER MATZAH

Illustrated by Paul Meisel
New York: Holiday House, 2010 | 978-0-8234-1952-4

4–8 YEARS

This fractured fairy tale takes the story of the Little Red Hen who wanted to make some bread and transposes it to a Little Red Hen who needs some matzah for the Jewish Passover holiday. As she plants the grain, cuts the wheat, carries the wheat to the mill, and prepares the matzah, she asks for help from her friends Sheep, Horse, and Dog, who all refuse. The lively text contains some Yiddish words, explained in a glossary at the back of the book. The barnyard and countryside scenes, illustrated in ink, watercolor, and pastel, tend toward the comical. And the little red hen? We should all have such a friend! She follows the words of the Passover Haggadah and invites the other animals to share her meal. Information about Passover and a recipe for matzah conclude the story. For a more traditional telling of the story see Jerry Pinkney's *The Little Red Hen* (Dial/Penguin, 2006).

Knutson, Barbara   4–8 YEARS
LOVE AND ROAST CHICKEN: A TRICKSTER TALE FROM THE ANDES MOUNTAINS
Illustrated by Barbara Knutson
Minneapolis: Carolrhoda, 2004 | 978-1-57505-657-9 | library binding

Appealing illustrations and a delightful story combine in this South American tale. A guinea pig tricks a fox several times with his cunning and quick thinking, always finding a way to turn bad situations to his favor. The artwork of mountains and alfalfa fields, and the costumes worn by the main character, Cuy, and the humans in the story, reflect the Andean setting. Note how the illustrations make use of distance and closeness to provide contrast and perspective. The text takes on a storytelling mode, which makes it a natural for read-alouds. A glossary of Spanish words with pronunciations appears at the back of the book. An author's note provides further information on South America, trickster tales, and guinea pigs. Complement with Virginia Hamilton's *Bruh Rabbit and the Tar Baby Girl* (Scholastic, 2003), a similar story in the African American tradition.

Langton, Jane   4–9 YEARS
SAINT FRANCIS AND THE WOLF
Illustrated by Ilse Plume
Boston: David R. Godine, 2007 | 978-1-56792-320-9

The legend of the wolf of Gubbio arose from the gentle ways of the real Saint Francis of Assisi, who was known for his kindness and generosity to all living things. In this story, a wolf terrorizes the people of Gubbio until they are prisoners in their homes. Francis promises to speak to the wolf, who listens to him and then changes his ways. The detailed illustrations, each set on its own page across from the text, feature fine lines and jewel colors. Each piece is framed, most as rectangles, but with diamond, circular, oval, and other more complicated shapes, too. The effect is one of viewing a fine painting on a wall, with the accompanying text to the side. The same legend told in a very different style is Richard Egielski's *Saint Francis and the Wolf* (Laura Geringer/HarperCollins, 2005).

Lunge-Larsen, Lise **4–8 YEARS**
NOAH'S MITTENS: THE STORY OF FELT
Illustrated by Matthew Trueman
Boston: Houghton Mifflin, 2006 | 978-0-618-32950-2

Who knew that Noah discovered how to make felt while aboard the ark? Concentrating on the sheep and what happens to their matted fleece with heat and friction, this lively rendering of the familiar Bible story entertains as it teaches a few facts about this fabric. The comical illustrations of pencil, gouache, acrylics, and collage portray Noah, the animals, and his family members as appealing characters. Scenes in the ark feature wood-bordered illustrations set against greenish blue water, playing up the enclosed feeling of life cooped up with creatures. Notice the beautiful texture of the animals, especially the sheep, both their fleece and their felt. A note on the origins of felt concludes the book.

MacDonald, Margaret Read, reteller
MABELA THE CLEVER
Illustrated by Tim Coffey
Morton Grove, IL: Albert Whitman, 2001 | 978-0-8075-4903-2 | paper

A tale from the Limba people of Africa, this story features a mouse who listens to her father's advice. When a cat promises membership in a secret Cat Club if the mice walk in single file and do not look back, Mabela soon discovers why the cat wants to be at the end of the line. Soon she is the only mouse left, as she suspected. When the cat pounces, she escapes and liberates the rest of the mice. The acrylic illustrations on paper textured with gesso create animals, vegetation, and thatched houses that look as if they would be soft, or smooth, or scratchy if felt. The illustrations, and sometimes the text, are bordered with a geometric pattern showing African influences. This book would make a wonderful introduction to folklore, especially the folklore of Africa. A classic story in which the smallest creature is the smartest.

MacDonald, Margaret Read, reteller **4–9 YEARS**
TUNJUR! TUNJUR! TUNJUR!
A PALESTINIAN FOLKTALE
Illustrated by Alik Arzoumanian
Tarrytown, NY: Marshall Cavendish, 2006 | 978-0-7614-5225-6

A lively little cooking pot becomes the child of a woman, who allows her little one to roll around their town. The title reflects the sound that the pot makes rolling on the cobbled street. After the pot convinces those she meets to fill her with honey and then again with jewelry, she refuses to let her lid be opened and gets into trouble with some influential townspeople. She eventually learns not to steal, which is the moral of the story. The richly colored illustrations, rendered in acrylics, depict stylized people and a pot with facial features. Illustrations covering two full pages present broad views of the woman's house and the little pot's travels; a narrow border of geometric or floral design in a coordinating color frame other single-page illustrations. Middle Eastern clothes, architecture, and design elements suffuse the story with an authentic air.

McDermott, Gerald   **4–8 YEARS**
PIG-BOY: A TRICKSTER TALE FROM HAWAI'I
Illustrated by Gerald McDermott
New York: Harcourt/Houghton Mifflin Harcourt, 2009 | 978-0-15-216590-1

Richly colored illustrations in textured gouache, colored pencil, and pastel delight the eye. Exciting text reads with the cadences of storytelling. Together they tell the tale of this trickster-hero of Hawaiian myth. The use of size provides interesting contrasts: as Pig-Boy eats and grows, he becomes large on the page; when he nestles in the arms of Grandmother or approaches the goddess Pele, he is small. Although this little pig bristles with hair and dirt and mischief, he comes across as lovable. The comical illustrations go a long way toward presenting him as cute, rather than ugly. The gorgeously colored artwork captures the beauty of the islands, while the story includes such crowd pleasers as magic, outsmarting the king, and a pig sailing a boat. An author's note at the beginning provides the background on the Pig-Boy tales.

McGill, Alice   **6–10 YEARS**
WAY UP AND OVER EVERYTHING
Illustrated by Jude Daly
Boston: Houghton Mifflin, 2008 | 978-0-618-38796-0

Can the desire for freedom be so strong that a person can fly away from a horrible situation? In this folktale that comes from the oral traditions of African Americans, slaves *can* step into the sky and fly away. The watercolor illustrations, in folk art style, are spare yet colorful, with shades of brown in skin and land, blue in water, and green in trees, and with splashes of bright color in clothing. The text, told by a girl who heard it passed down by female relatives, relates the story of how five slaves, newly brought from Africa, whirled and flew away from the overseer and master. Hope triumphs over sorrow in this fine African American folktale. A note at the end provides information on African slaves and their flying stories.

Mora, Pat   **4–8 YEARS**
DOÑA FLOR: A TALL TALE ABOUT A GIANT WOMAN WITH A GREAT BIG HEART
Illustrated by Raul Colón
New York: Alfred A. Knopf, 2005 | 978-0-375-82337-4

Doña Flor comes from the Paul Bunyan tall tale tradition: a giant who is strong and uses her power for good. When she finds that her neighbors have been terrified by a mountain lion that they hear roaring, she sets out to find it. How surprised she is when all she discovers is a small cat growling through a big log. She befriends the cat and soon all is peaceful again. The book itself is tall, as befits its subject matter. The large illustrations make the most of the contrast between Doña Flor and the tiny villagers and animals. Muted illustrations have a pointillist feel and lend themselves well to the contrasting forces of gentleness and power that occur in each picture. With some Spanish words scattered throughout, *Doña Flor* is a good introduction to the tales of this culture. Discover Paul Bunyan's sister's story in *Paula Bunyan* (Farrar Straus Giroux, 2009) by Phyllis Root.

Morales, Yuyi   **4–8 YEARS**
JUST IN CASE: A TRICKSTER TALE AND SPANISH ALPHABET BOOK
Illustrated by Yuyi Morales
New York: Neal Porter/Roaring Brook, 2008 | 978-1-59643-329-8

Señor Calavera, the Grim Reaper of *Just a Minute: A Trickster Tale and Counting Book* (Chronicle, 2003) by Morales, rattles back again, ready to go to Grandma Beetle's birthday party. For a skeleton, Señor Calavera is rather cute: he has flowers on his eyeballs, a pert upside-down heart for a nose surrounded by red jewels, and purple eyebrows. But his handsome self cannot be enough; he must take a gift. Aided by Zelmiro the Ghost, he collects one item for each letter of the alphabet. The illustrations, rich and colorful, provide plenty to look at on each page. The Spanish name appears next to each item in the A-to-Z array—for example, *un acordeón* for an accordion. A mood of hurry-hurry permeates the pictures, as Señor Calavera rushes to get to the party, where Grandma Beetle receives the best present of all.

Nishizuka, Koko   **4–8 YEARS**
THE BECKONING CAT
Illustrated by Rosanne Litzinger
New York: Holiday House, 2009 | 978-0-8234-2051-3

When Yohei, a poor young boy living in a Japanese fishing village, feeds a stray cat, he has no idea what the consequences will be. A few days later, he finds that villagers are coming to him to buy fish, persuaded by the cat beckoning with her little paw. Eventually Yohei is able to open a shop. The illustrations, delicately done in watercolor, colored pencil, ink, and gouache, portray Yohei and the other characters in traditional costumes, which set the story long ago. Bright colors and large character close-ups make it easy to share this book with a group. And the cat? Just adorable! The last page relates how she became a symbol of good luck and, as a porcelain statue, ubiquitous in stores in Asia. A beautiful folktale, ideal for sharing with young children.

Nolen, Jerdine   **5–8 YEARS**
THUNDER ROSE
Illustrated by Kadir Nelson
Orlando: Silver Whistle/Harcourt, 2003 | 978-0-15-216472-0

With a crash of thunder and a flash of lightning, baby Rose is born, and immediately her parents know that she is special. She speaks formally and displays uncanny strength, even as a baby. Set in the Old West, this folktale features an African American cowgirl who can accomplish amazing feats. For those who always wondered where barbed wire came from, it's an invention of Thunder Rose, named after her little sister Barbara! From tracking down desperadoes to controlling a tornado, this Rose is one tough cowgirl. The illustrations—oil, watercolor, and pencil—evoke amazement in some instances and aw-shucks everyday life in others. Young girls will admire Rose's strength and courage.

Osborne, Will, and Mary Pope Osborne   **4–8 YEARS**
SLEEPING BOBBY
Illustrated by Giselle Potter
New York: Anne Schwartz/Atheneum, 2005 | 978-0-689-87668-4

An alternative version of the Sleeping Beauty fairy tale, this story does some gender-bending and features a Bobby instead of a Beauty. The rest of the story follows the traditional plot, except that a beautiful princess comes to awaken the handsome prince from his hundred-year spell. Simple yet delightful illustrations use pencil, ink, gouache, gesso, and watercolor. Parents and teachers of the very young may appreciate the fact that the wicked old woman who puts the spell on Bobby does not look particularly scary. Endpapers feature young women trying to get through the thorny hedge during the hundred-year sleep, following up on that particular illustration in the story. Those who love happily ever after tales with a twist will appreciate this story. Readers may also enjoy the Osborne-Potter collaboration on *The Brave Little Seamstress* (2002) and *Kate and the Beanstalk* (2000). Another take on the story is Bruce Hale's *Snoring Beauty* (Harcourt, 2008).

Palatini, Margie   **4–8 YEARS**
LOUSY ROTTEN STINKIN' GRAPES
Illustrated by Barry Moser
New York: Simon & Schuster, 2009 | 978-0-689-80246-1

This version of the Aesop's fable begs to be read out loud with sass and comic timing. Fox, quite full of himself, thinks he has devised the perfect plan to reach the
beautiful purple grapes. As he enlists one animal after another to do his bidding,
he still cannot get to the fruit. The realistic watercolor illustrations lend humor
to the quest, as does the text. Fox continually refers to his cleverness, even as the
other animals come up with good ideas which he dismisses. This Fox has personality, and adult readers who like to ham it up will find a perfect vehicle here for
their talents. Young listeners who love animal stories or humorous stories are in
for a treat.

Pinkney, Jerry   **4–8 YEARS**
THE LION & THE MOUSE
Illustrated by Jerry Pinkney
New York: Little, Brown, 2009 | 978-0-316-01356-7

This nearly wordless book retells Aesop's fable of the mouse who, because of a lion's
earlier kindness, now rescues him by gnawing off the ropes that hold the king of the
beasts ensnared. The animals, realistically rendered in gorgeous pencil, watercolor,
and colored pencil illustrations, inhabit the African Serengeti, according to a note at
the end of the book. Vegetation, additional animals, and safari hunters contribute to
the fully rounded scenes that largely feature the lion and the mouse. The only words
that appear are the animal sounds of the owl, the mice, and the lion, and the motor
sounds of the hunters' jeep. What a marvelous book for a storyteller to use, or for a
child who enjoys telling the story from the pictures. The winner of the 2010 Caldecott
Medal, *The Lion & the Mouse* displays Pinkney's storytelling skills and artistic excellence.

Poole, Amy Lowry, reteller   **4–9 YEARS**
THE PEA BLOSSOM
Illustrated by Amy Lowry Poole
New York: Holiday House, 2005 | 978-0-8234-2018-6 | paper

Based on a Hans Christian Andersen story, this tale is set in China, where the author
lived for a time. The spare yet evocative illustrations, delicate paintings on rice paper,
express just a touch of whimsy. Note the animal shapes to illustrate trees and ground.
The five peas in the shell exhibit interesting facial expressions as they talk about their
future lives. The four who have big plans end up being eaten, while the fifth, with a

Zen outlook, is content to be happy with whatever happens. He fulfills his destiny in helping a young girl get well. This book could be used in the study of traditional tales, as a science lesson in seeds and plant growth, for art instruction, or as a quiet book to enjoy by oneself.

San Souci, Robert D., reteller   **4–9 YEARS**
ROBIN HOOD AND THE GOLDEN ARROW
Illustrated by E.B. Lewis
New York: Orchard/Scholastic, 2010 | 978-0-439-62538-8 | library binding

The traditional tale of Robin Hood and the Merry Men of Sherwood Forest springs to life in this retelling. Who can resist the story of Robin and his band, which culminates in an archery contest where a disguised Robin bests the sheriff's favorite and wins the golden prize? Beautiful watercolor illustrations feature dominant colors of green and brown, with splashes of red, especially Robin's hood and shirt that he wears to the contest. Faces come across as very realistic, especially in the close-ups. The large size of the book matches the larger-than-life character of Robin Hood. An author's note at the end explains the origins of the story from a traditional British ballad. After reading this, it could be time to introduce the next generation to the classic 1938 film *The Adventures of Robin Hood,* starring Errol Flynn.

Santore, Charles   **5–10 YEARS**
THE SILK PRINCESS
Illustrated by Charles Santore
New York: Random House, 2007 | 978-0-375-83664-0

Based on a legend that stretches back to 2700 BC, the story of the princess who discovers a secret thread combines fantasy and reality. Princess Hsi-Ling Chi, confined like her mother to the Royal Palace and gardens, notices a cocoon that unravels when it falls in hot tea. With her mother's consent, she ventures away with the string to see how far it will go. After a nap, she meets a talking spider, a dragon, and an old man weaving thread. Or was that a dream? Either way, exciting events told in the text and sumptuously illustrated unfold until she journeys back to her mother with the secret of silk. The illustrations offer a wealth of variety in color, scene, and size of the main character. One especially effective page spread frames the old weaver and the princess with a border of leaves and pale silkworms, their trailing thread caught up by the old man's hand in the central illustration. A wonderful read-aloud for the study of ancient Chinese culture, legends, or simply a gripping tale.

Smith, Chris   **4–10 YEARS**
ONE CITY, TWO BROTHERS
Illustrated by Aurélia Fronty
Cambridge, MA: Barefoot, 2007 | 978-1-84686-042-3

From the Middle East comes this tale of brothers who share farm fields and the work of harvesting. Each brother secretly gives his sibling a larger portion of grain, until they discover what each is doing. The love and respect between the two consecrates the ground, where it is believed the city of Jerusalem began. Illustrations in acrylics bring a sense of the sacred to the story, with stylized drawings of people, buildings, and animals in rich hues of greens, yellows, and blues. The story itself is part of the oral tradition of many peoples, both Jews and Palestinian Arabs. This book can be used in many ways: as part of social studies, in the study of folktales, as an illustration of sharing and family love, or simply as a wonderful visual and aural treat to enjoy. Endpapers feature doves and hearts, which can also be found on some of the pages within.

Souhami, Jessica   **4–8 YEARS**
KING POM AND THE FOX
Illustrated by Jessica Souhami
London: Frances Lincoln, 2007 | 978-1-84507-365-7 | paper

Known as Puss in Boots in the West, this Chinese version introduces King Pom, short for *pomegranate tree*, which is the only item that Li Ming owns. With the help of a clever fox who is an expert at the art of convincing people, Li Ming acquires a palace and marries the emperor's daughter. The illustrations, in bold colors, are a collage of papers hand-painted with watercolor inks and graphite pencil. Their form and color allow them to stand out starkly on each page, with little detail, but a pleasing shape. Facial expressions and body positions convey emotion, while the depiction of movement, especially of animals, is thrilling. Notice especially the two-page spreads of the tiger leaping and the fox attacking an ogre-turned-bug. Listeners will cheer at the end as both Li Ming and the fox come out on top.

Spirin, Gennady   **4–8 YEARS**
A APPLE PIE
Illustrated by Gennady Spirin
New York: Philomel, 2005 | 978-0-399-23981-6

Based on an alphabet rhyme from the 1600s, this book features Spirin's marvelous watercolor illustrations. The Victorian setting and costumes create an old-fashioned feel to the active rhyme; the detail will give listeners much to peruse. Each page or two-page spread features a letter of the alphabet in both print and cursive, plus a two- or three-word phrase about the pie: "bit it," "cut it," and so on. A large letter centers the illustration on the page and the characters sit on it, jump from it, or are surrounded by it as a frame. The pie itself appears large in all the illustrations, and huge in some. Each page also contains an apple in the corner, introducing another common thread throughout the book. A beautiful rendition of an old nursery rhyme, this version could serve as an introductory ABC for young ones.

Squires, Janet   3–8 YEARS
THE GINGERBREAD COWBOY
Illustrated by Holly Berry
New York: Laura Geringer/HarperCollins, 2006 | 978-0-06-077863-7

Break out the ten-gallon hats and get ready for a Wild West version of the Little Gingerbread Man. In this retelling, a rancher's wife makes a gingerbread cowboy cookie, complete with hat, boots, and vest. True to form, he escapes the oven and runs as fast as he can out of the kitchen. Eventually a lizard, a roadrunner, javelinas, cattle, and cowboys chase after him until he meets the coyote that promises rescue. Even though the rancher's wife tries to lasso him, the gingerbread cowboy crosses the river on the coyote's nose, and everyone knows how *that* will end. The last page shows the rancher and his wife and a surprise guest back in the kitchen making more gingerbread cowboys. On most pages, illustrations with a Southwest feel cover the entire two-page spread, perfect for group read-alouds. For other gingerbread people, see Margie Palatini's *Bad Boys Get Cookie!* (HarperCollins, 2006) and Jan Brett's *Gingerbread Friends* (Putnam, 2008). A Jewish version by Lisa Shulman is *The Matzo Ball Boy* (Dutton, 2005). The gingerbread boy's sister is featured in *The Gingerbread Girl* by Lisa Campbell Ernst (Dutton, 2006).

Sweet, Melissa   4–8 YEARS
CARMINE: A LITTLE MORE RED
Illustrated by Melissa Sweet
Boston: Houghton Mifflin, 2005 | 978-0-618-38794-6

An excellent example of an alphabet book built into a story, this takeoff on Little Red Riding Hood contains some words that might not readily come to mind for this tale. *Haiku*? *Nincompoop*? *Yodel*? Yes, they are all in here, and they work. The mixed-media illustrations feature the color red, of course, but it does not overpower the greens, browns, blues, and yellows. The endpapers at the front feature labeled and unlabeled objects in shades of red—alphabet pasta (which figures into the story) spells out names on the labels—and the endpapers at the back feature additional colors, more alphabet pasta, and a recipe for Granny's alphabet soup. Unlike other Little Reds, this story ends happily for all, even the wolf. An interesting contrast is Ann Whitford Paul's version, *Tortuga in Trouble* (Holiday House, 2009). See, too, Gail Carson Levine's *Betsy Red Hoodie* (HarperCollins, 2010), in which the wolf is a shepherd to a flock of wisecracking sheep. An African version of the tale appears in Niki Daly's *Pretty Salma* (Clarion, 2007). Jerry Pinkney's take stays true in title and telling: *Little Red Riding Hood* (Little, Brown, 2007).

Taback, Simms   3–8 YEARS
THIS IS THE HOUSE THAT JACK BUILT
Illustrated by Simms Taback
New York: G.P. Putnam's Sons, 2002 | 978-0-399-23488-0

The traditional tale of Jack's House appears here, exploding in color and humorous detail. The page about the cheese features nine different types, complete with descriptive comments on their smell. The page with the dog uses collage to show several types of dog food, a dish, and biscuits. Agreements, summonses, and other legal documents litter the page introducing the judge. This theme carries throughout the book, including the endpapers, which are packed with small paintings of houses over newspaper real estate ads. The words in bright colors, as the cumulative story progresses, become more and more packed on the page. The collage illustrations add to the manic mood. A comical take on a familiar rhyme, this version adds a final section that features the artist.

VanHecke, Susan, reteller   4–8 YEARS
AN APPLE PIE FOR DINNER
Illustrated by Carol Baicker-McKee
Tarrytown, NY: Marshall Cavendish, 2009 | 978-0-7614-5452-6

Based on an English folktale, this story follows an old woman who wishes to make an apple pie but has no apples. She takes a walk and trades what she has with various characters along the way until she finds someone who can trade for apples. In the end, all the characters enjoy apple pie seated at her table. Bas-reliefs of baked clay and mixed media project a three-dimensional look to the illustrations. The folksy charm of the illustrations suits the tale. Check the details, such as cuts in green material to represent grass and the clasp on Granny Smith's shawl of a Granny Smith apple. A recipe for apple pie appropriately ends the book. Bobbi Miller's *One Fine Trade* (Holiday House, 2009) presents a backwoods version.

Ward, Jennifer   **4–8 YEARS**
THERE WAS AN OLD MONKEY
WHO SWALLOWED A FROG
Illustrated by Steve Gray
Tarrytown, NY: Marshall Cavendish, 2010 | 978-0-7614-5580-6

A googly-eyed, big-eared monkey takes on the title role in this version of "There was an old lady who swallowed a fly." Here, the monkey swallows all sorts of rain forest animals, not to mention some cocoa. As the rhyme progresses, the manic illustrations in digital media keep piling on, until the final page is stuffed full of creatures. Listeners will enjoy finishing the sentences as they repeat, and seeing what animal is next to be swallowed. The jungle scenes abound in green, while the creatures represent a rainbow of colors, crisp lines, and goofy expressions. Great good fun to read and hear. Compare to *There Was an Old Monster!* (Orchard/Scholastic, 2009) by Rebecca, Adrian, and Ed Emberley, also full of animals and rich colors.

Willey, Margaret   **4–8 YEARS**
CLEVER BEATRICE
Illustrated by Heather Solomon
New York: Atheneum/Simon & Schuster, 2001 | 978-0-689-83254-3

Michigan's Upper Peninsula becomes the setting for this Canadian conte, a story told with humor and exaggeration. Beatrice, known by her village neighbors to be a quick thinker, visits a rich giant in order to help her poor mother. Through a series of bets, and without having to prove her strength, she outsmarts the giant, who is so sure of his own. In the end, she wins a bag full of coins and the admiration of her mother. Readers and listeners will delight in this fearless little girl's use of brains over brawn. The illustrations, rendered in watercolor, collage, acrylic, and oils, bring out the rich browns, reds, oranges, and greens of the forests. The endpapers contain colorful maps of Northern Wisconsin and Michigan, some of the Great Lakes, and a bit of Canada, with characters from the book scattered throughout. For another clever character, read *Jack Outwits the Giants* by Paul Brett Johnson (Simon & Schuster, 2002).

Suggested Resources

For Further Research into Picture Books

These books and organizations will aid teachers, librarians, writers, and parents who want to know more about picture books and their uses. The titles are, for the most part, published within the last ten years, although the list includes several classics as well. In cases where the entire text is not devoted to picture books, I have indicated which chapters or sections cover them.

Amoss, Berthe, and Eric Suben. *Writing and Illustrating Children's Books for Publication: Two Perspectives.* Rev ed. Cincinnati: Writer's Digest, 2005.
Authors with backgrounds in writing, illustrating, teaching, and editing offer a short course on all aspects of children's literature, with many examples from picture books.

Asher, Sandy. *Writing It Right! How Successful Children's Authors Revise and Sell Their Stories.* West Redding, CT: Writer's Institute, 2009.
The section on picture books examines the drafts that went into the making of four of these books, plus interviews with the authors.

Association for Library Service to Children, a division of the American Library Association. www.ala.org/alsc.
ALSC bestows the Caldecott, Coretta Scott King, Belpré, Schneider Family, and other book awards and advocates on behalf of reading and books.

Bader, Barbara. *American Picturebooks from Noah's Ark to the Beast Within.* New York: Macmillan, 1976.

An excellent source for the study of the history of this form. Covers the famous authors and artists, styles, publishers, and social change.

Bang, Molly. *Picture This: How Pictures Work.* San Francisco: SeaStar, 2000.
How do shape, color, size, and layout "make" a picture? Bang explains, with ample illustrations of her simple yet emotionally complex shapes.

Bomhold, Catharine, and Terri E. Elder. *Twice Upon a Time: A Guide to Fractured, Altered, and Retold Folk and Fairy Tales.* Westport, CT: Libraries Unlimited, 2008.
An annotated list of versions of twenty-seven common tales, with notes as to the country or culture of origin. Includes title, author, illustrator, country/culture, and motif indexes.

Broman, Jennifer. *Storytime Action! 2,000+ Ideas for Making 500 Picture Books Interactive.* New York: Neal-Schuman, 2003.
———. *More Storytime Action.* New York: Neal-Schuman, 2009.
Bring sound and motion to storytimes in public and school libraries with these ideas.

Cooperative Children's Book Center. www.education.wisc.edu/ccbc.
A wealth of information for librarians, teachers, day care providers, and students of children's literature. The CCBC also presents the annual Charlotte Zolotow Award.

Edwards, Gail, and Judith Saltman. *Picturing Canada: A History of Canadian Children's Illustrated Books and Publishing.* University of Toronto, 2010.
A comprehensive examination of children's literature in Canada, especially illustrated books, 1800s to the present. With information on major publishers, authors, illustrators, awards, and cultural identity.

Eric Carle Museum of Picture Book Art. Amherst, MA. www.carle museum.org.

Evans, Dilys. *Show & Tell: Exploring the Fine Art of Children's Book Illustration.* San Francisco: Chronicle, 2008.
Learn how twelve illustrators found their calling and how they work; includes lots of illustrations.

Evans, Janet, ed. *Talking Beyond the Page: Reading and Responding to Picturebooks.* London: Routledge, 2009.
A collection of scholarly essays on children's understanding and response to books, with chapters on endpapers, frames, narrative, and immigrant children's responses.

Giblin, James Cross. *The Giblin Guide to Writing Children's Books.* 4th ed. West Redding, CT: Writer's Institute, 2005.
Practical advice from a children's author and editor. Three chapters specifically concern picture books.

Hearn, Michael Patrick, Trinkett Clark, and H. Nichols B. Clark. *Myth, Magic, and Mystery: One Hundred Years of American Children's Book Illustration.* Boulder, CO: Roberts Rinehart, in cooperation with the Chrysler Museum of Art, 1996.
Revel in the variety of styles and subjects in this history, beginning with the British forebears of children's book illustration.

Kirk, Connie Ann. *Companion to American Children's Picture Books.* Westport, CT: Greenwood, 2005.
More than four hundred entries on important books, authors, illustrators, and related topics.

Knowles, Liz, and Martha Smith. *Understanding Diversity through Novels and Picture Books.* Westport, CT: Libraries Unlimited, 2007.
A guide to literature and resources for teachers and librarians, with chapters on a variety of ethnic groups, as well as ageism, gender, sexual orientation, religion, and other issues.

Lima, Carolyn W., and Rebecca L. Thomas. *A to Zoo: Subject Access to Children's Picture Books.* 8th ed. Providence, NJ: R.R. Bowker, 2010.
A standard reference tool in libraries, this extensive subject guide provides bibliographic information, title index, and illustrator index.

Marantz, Sylvia, and Ken Marantz. *Multicultural Picturebooks: Art for Illuminating Our World.* 2d ed. Lanham, MD: Scarecrow, 2005.
Find annotated listings of picture books covering Asia, the Middle East, Africa, the Americas, and cross-cultural. Includes original tales, folk tales, and immigrant experiences.

Marcus, Leonard S. *Ways of Telling: Conversations on the Art of the Picture Book.* New York: Dutton, 2002.
Children's literature scholar Marcus interviews fourteen writers and illustrators, including some of the biggest names in picture books, such as Zolotow, Sendak, and Pinkney.

Matulka, Denise I. *A Picture Book Primer: Understanding and Using Picture Books.* Westport, CT: Libraries Unlimited, 2008.
Discover the anatomy, genres, development, issues, and uses of picture books in this comprehensive guide. Companion website: www.picturingbooks.com.

Mazza Museum. University of Findlay, OH. www.findlay.edu/offices/resources/mazza.

McCannon, Desdemona, Sue Thornton, and Yadzia Williams. *The Encyclopedia of Writing and Illustrating Children's Books.* Philadelphia: Running Press, 2008.
How is a children's book created? This heavily illustrated volume covers word and picture, fiction and nonfiction. Much of the content is applicable to picture books, especially the many sections on illustration.

National Center for Children's Illustrated Literature. Abilene, TX. www.nccil.org.

Nikolajeva, Maria, and Carole Scott. *How Picturebooks Work.* New York: Routledge, 2006.

In-depth look at how pictures and words come together by analyzing setting, characters, narrative, language, and more. Uses American and Swedish picture books as examples.

Nodelman, Perry. *Words about Pictures: The Narrative Art of Children's Picture Books.* Athens: University of Georgia, 1988.

This scholarly, oft-cited book covers such concepts as style as meaning, codes and symbols, the depiction of action and time, and the relationship of pictures and words.

Pantaleo, Sylvia. *Exploring Student Response to Contemporary Picturebooks.* University of Toronto, 2008.

A scholarly analysis of children's interpretations of books, based on a four-year study of first and fifth graders.

Paul, Ann Whitford. *Writing Picture Books: A Hands-On Guide from Story Creation to Publication.* Cincinnati, OH: Writer's Digest, 2009.

Although geared to children's writers, anyone interested in the structure of picture books, importance of words, and characteristics of the reader will find much to learn.

Polette, Nancy J. *Reading the World with Picture Books.* Santa Barbara, CA: Libraries Unlimited/ABC-CLIO, 2010.

For over one hundred countries, an annotated list of picture books, plus activities to fulfill national standards in language arts and social studies.

———. *Teaching Thinking Skills with Picture Books, K–3.* Westport, CT: Teacher Ideas/Libraries Unlimited, 2007.

Reproducible classroom activities for teachers and school librarians to use with classic and recent picture books.

Salisbury, Martin. *Illustrating Children's Books: Creating Pictures for Publication.* Hauppauge, NY: Barron's, 2004.

Covers the art of drawing; materials; making characters come alive; and the illustration of picture books, chapter books, and nonfiction.

Shulevitz, Uri. *Writing with Pictures: How to Write and Illustrate Children's Books.* New York: Watson-Guptill, 1985.

Well illustrated with numerous line drawings and reproductions, this book could be used as a text for aspiring writer/illustrators.

Sipe, Lawrence R., and Sylvia Pantaleo, eds. *Postmodern Picturebooks: Play, Parody, and Self-Referentiality.* New York: Routledge/Taylor & Francis, 2008.

A collection of scholarly articles by professors of children's literature. A good overview of postmodernism in the picture book.

Spitz, Ellen Handler. *Inside Picture Books.* New Haven: Yale University, 1999.
A scholar in art, psychology, and culture, Spitz looks at classic children's books and how they affect children.

Stanton, Joseph. *The Important Books: Children's Picture Books as Art and Literature.* Lanham, MD: Scarecrow, 2005.
Separate chapters explore the words and art of books by Margaret Wise Brown, Arnold Lobel, Donald Hall and Barbara Cooney, Maurice Sendak, William Joyce, and Chris Van Allsburg.

Stephens, Claire Gatrell. *Picture This! Using Picture Story Books for Character Education in the Classroom.* Westport, CT: Libraries Unlimited, 2004.
Comprehensive lesson plans for teachers in grades K–8 to teach character and integrate the lessons of the books into their curriculum.

Sutherland, Zena. *Children & Books.* 9th ed. New York: Longman, 1997.
The classic text on children's literature, covering history, types, authors and illustrators, and the use of children's literature in the classroom.

Vardell, Sylvia M. *Children's Literature in Action: A Librarian's Guide.* Westport, CT: Libraries Unlimited, 2008.
See especially chapters on "Picture Books" and "Traditional Tales" for introductions to these types.

Withrow, Steven, and Lesley Breen Withrow. *Illustrating Children's Picture Books.* Cincinnati: Writer's Digest, 2009.
Solid instruction supplemented with case studies and interviews with experts, well illustrated throughout in color. A section on digital illustrations provides up-to-date advice.

Zipes, Jack, ed. *The Norton Anthology of Children's Literature: The Traditions in English.* New York: W.W. Norton, 2005.
A hefty volume (2,471 pages) that goes back to the 1600s and Comenius's Orbis Pictus. Divided into headings such as fairy tales, animal fables, science fiction, comics, and verse. See especially section on picture books, which includes representative illustrations.

Appendix 1
Picture Books about Art

These books revel in the wonder of museums, replete with well-known works of art, and in the magic of creating art—its inspirations and its process.

Anholt, Laurence. *Cézanne and the Apple Boy.* Hauppauge, NY: Barron's, 2009.
   A young boy helps his father, the reclusive artist Paul Cézanne, who struggles to have his art taken seriously.
Baker, Sharon Reiss. *A Nickel, a Trolley, a Treasure House.* Illustrated by Beth Peck. New York: Viking, 2007.
   Inspired by an understanding teacher, a boy in early 1900s New York visits a museum and recognizes his own artistic talent.
Beard, Alex. *Monkey See, Monkey Draw.* New York: Abrams, 2011.
   A group of energetic monkeys discover the fun and possibilities of creating paintings from handprints and footprints.
Browne, Anthony. *The Shape Game.* New York: Farrar Straus Giroux, 2003.
   A young boy tours a museum, and the works of art become a springboard for family discussion in this humorous story.
Haseley, Dennis. *Twenty Heartbeats.* Illustrated by Ed Young. New York: Neal Porter/Roaring Brook, 2008.
   Depicted as an old Chinese legend, this story portrays a famous painter commissioned by a rich man to create a painting of his favorite horse.

Hogrogian, Nonny. *Cool Cat.* New York: Neal Porter/Roaring Brook, 2009.
Helped by various animals, a cat changes their landscape from dull to colorful in this wordless picture book.

Johnson, Angela. *Lily Brown's Paintings.* Illustrated by E.B. Lewis. New York: Orchard/Scholastic, 2007.
A young African American girl creates art based on the world she sees and the magic she imagines.

Larsen, Andrew. *The Imaginary Garden.* Illustrated by Irene Luxbacher. Toronto: Kids Can, 2009.
A little girl and her grandfather paint a colorful garden that enlivens their black-and-white apartments.

Lichtenheld, Tom. *Bridget's Beret.* New York: Christy Ottaviano/Henry Holt, 2010.
A young girl loses her inspiration when she loses her artist's beret.

Magoon, Scott. *Hugo & Miles in I've Painted Everything!* Boston: Houghton Mifflin, 2007.
Two friends take a trip to Paris, where the museums and the atmosphere inspire one of them to return to his painting.

Maltbie, P. I. *Picasso and Minou.* Illustrated by Pau Estrada. Watertown, MA: Charlesbridge, 2005.
Picasso's pet cat helps him move from his Blue Period to his Rose Period, which enables him to support himself and keep on painting.

Mayhew, James. *Katie's Sunday Afternoon.* New York: Orchard/Scholastic, 2004.
At a gallery, a young girl climbs into one painting after another, where she meets the characters portrayed. See also *Katie and the Sunflowers* (2000), *Katie and the Spanish Princess* (2006), and *Katie and the Water Lily Pond* (2010).

McDonnell, Patrick. *Art.* New York: Little, Brown, 2006.
A young boy named Art creates art in this celebration of the techniques, subjects, and appreciation of artistic endeavor.

Montanari, Eva. *Chasing Degas.* New York: Abrams, 2009.
A young ballerina tries desperately to find the painter whose bag was mixed up with hers, and she meets famous artists in 1870s Paris along the way.

———. *The Crocodile's True Colors.* New York: Watson-Guptill, 2002.
As various animals attempt to portray a crocodile in their art, readers learn about Expressionism, Cubism, Dadaism, and other artistic styles.

Pericoli, Matteo. *Tommaso and the Missing Line.* New York: Alfred A. Knopf, 2008.
Bright orange lines stand out in black-and-white illustrations as a boy searches throughout his town for the line missing from his drawing.

Pfister, Marcus. *Henri, Egg Artiste.* Translated by J. Alison James. New York: North-South, 2005.

An Easter egg-painting rabbit decides to try something different, which results in art inspired by famous artists.

Reynolds, Peter H. *The Dot.* Cambridge, MA: Candlewick, 2003.

Convinced that she cannot draw, a young girl begins with a dot and then is inspired to paint with that theme.

———. *Ish.* Cambridge, MA: Candlewick, 2004.

A negative remark by his brother makes Ramon give up drawing, until his sister restores his confidence.

Scieszka, Jon. *Seen Art?* Illustrated by Lane Smith. New York: Viking and the Museum of Modern Art, 2005.

With wordplay and reproductions of famous artistic works, this story of a young boy looking for his friend Art also takes him into the Museum of Modern Art to discover art.

Spiro, Ruth. *Lester Fizz, Bubble-Gum Artist.* Illustrated by Thor Wickstrom. New York: Dutton, 2008.

Although Lester doesn't seem to fit in with his family of artists, he finds his talent in this story filled with famous works of art.

Thomson, Bill. *Chalk.* Tarrytown, NY: Marshall Cavendish, 2010.

In this wordless picture book, a group of children make chalk drawings that mysteriously become real.

Tougas, Chris. *Art's Supplies.* Victoria, BC: Orca, 2008.

Pencils, markers, scissors, and other supplies come to colorful and humorous life.

Wallace, Nancy Elizabeth. *Look! Look! Look!* Tarrytown, NY: Marshall Cavendish, 2006.

As a mouse family discusses a famous painting on a postcard, readers learn about pattern, color, line, and other artistic elements.

Wiesner, David. *Art & Max.* Boston: Clarion/Houghton Mifflin Harcourt, 2010.

Max wants to paint, and things get quickly out of control in this colorful adventure.

Appendix 2
Self-Referential Picture Books

As a type of postmodern picture book, the following titles break through the traditional dimensions of the book. Both words and pictures may be involved: the author speaks directly to the reader, or the illustrations feature characters who escape the confines of their space, as if they know they are in a book.

Burleigh, Robert. *I Love Going Through this Book.* Illustrated by Dan Yaccarino. New York: Joanna Cotler/HarperCollins, 2001.
A boy walks through a book from beginning to end with some animal friends that burst through pages, hang from a rip, and even nibble on a torn page.
Child, Lauren. *Beware of the Storybook Wolves.* New York: Arthur A. Levine/ Scholastic, 2000.
Fierce animals from his bedtime story involve young Herb in an adventure with other characters who have escaped their books.
———. *Who's Afraid of the Big Bad Book?* New York: Hyperion, 2002.
Herb is back again, this time having fallen into a book that he had cut and colored in, to the frustration of its characters.
Czekaj, Jef. *Cat Secrets.* New York: Balzer + Bray/HarperCollins, 2011.
The cats in this book address the reader personally, as they insist that only cats can read the book.
Gerstein, Mordicai. *A Book.* New York: Roaring Brook, 2009.
A young girl in a family that lives in a book tries to figure out her story as she encounters various genres.

Gravett, Emily. *Wolves*. New York: Simon & Schuster, 2005.
   A rabbit checks out a library book about wolves that become very much a part of the story.
Jeffers, Oliver. *The Incredible Book Eating Boy*. New York: Philomel, 2006.
   Henry eats books and becomes extremely smart, but a crisis forces him to find a different way to appreciate them (never mind the bite marks at the end!).
Kanninen, Barbara. *A Story with Pictures*. Illustrated by Lynn Rowe Reed. New York: Holiday House, 2007.
   Readers will learn what makes up a story as they encounter characters, problems, settings, and a plot with lots of action.
Lehman, Barbara. *The Red Book*. Boston: Houghton Mifflin, 2004.
   In this wordless story, a girl finds a book that, when opened, transports her from a snowy city to a sunny island.
Lendler, Ian. *An Undone Fairy Tale*. Illustrated by Whitney Martin. New York: Simon & Schuster, 2005.
   As a fairy tale is told, the author interrupts to introduce the illustrator, comment on reading ability, and ask the reader not to turn the page.
Lewis, Jill. *Don't Read this Book!* Illustrated by Deborah Allwright. Wilton, CT: Tiger Tales/ME Media, 2009.
   A king and a story writer collaborate to create a story, which the king insists that the reader not read.
Muntean, Michaela. *Do Not Open this Book!* Illustrated by Pascal Lemaitre. New York: Scholastic, 2006.
   While the story is being written, a small pig begs the reader not to open the book or turn the pages.
Perry, John. *The Book that Eats People*. Illustrated by Mark Fearing. Berkeley: Tricycle, 2009.
   Humorous and scary in equal measure, this story tells the tale of the people eaten by this particular book.
Schwarz, Viviane. *There Are No Cats in this Book*. Somerville, MA: Candlewick, 2010.
   Three cats, speaking to the reader, announce their intention to leave the book, which they do, although they return with friends at the end.
Stevenson, James. *No Laughing, No Smiling, No Giggling*. New York: Frances Foster/Farrar Straus Giroux, 2004.
   A pig and a crocodile present the rules for reading, which they then enforce on the reader through the course of several short stories.
Watt, Mélanie. *Chester*. Toronto: Kids Can, 2007.
   A fat cat takes over the telling and illustrating of a story, which turns into a battle with the author.

———. *Chester's Masterpiece.* Toronto: Kids Can, 2010.

Chester is back again to frustrate the author as they go back and forth about how the story should look and how it should be told.

———. *Have I Got a Book for You!* Toronto: Kids Can, 2009.

Salesman Al Foxword talks directly to the reader as he attempts to sell books in this story.

Whatley, Bruce. *Wait! No Paint!* New York: HarperCollins, 2001.

The tale of the three pigs veers into humorous territory as the illustrator and his tools become part of the story.

Wiesner, David. *The Three Pigs.* New York: Clarion, 2001.

The pigs and the wolf escape the pages and find their way into another story in this Caldecott Medal winner.

Illustration Credits

Figure 2.1 (page 25):From *Turtle Girl* by Carole Crowe. Illustrated by Jim Postier. Illustration copyright © 2008 by Jim Postier. Published by Boyds Mills Press, Inc. Used with permission.

Figure 2.2 (page 29): From *A Day with Dad* by Bo R. Holmberg. Illustrated by Eva Eriksson. Illustration copyright © 2008 by Eva Eriksson. Reproduced by permission of the publisher, Candlewick Press, Somerville, MA.

Figure 2.3 (page 35): From *Looking Like Me* by Walter Dean Myers. Illustrated by Christopher Myers. Text copyright © Walter Dean Myers, 2009. Art copyright © Christopher Myers, 2009. First published by Egmont, USA, 2009. Used with permission.

Figure 2.4 (page 38): From *All in a Day* by Cynthia Rylant. Illustrated by Nikki McClure. Illustration © 2009 by Nikki McClure. Published by Abrams Books for Young Readers, an imprint of Harry N. Abrams, Inc., New York. All rights reserved.

Figure 2.5 (page 40): From *Monsoon Afternoon* by Kashmira Sheth. Illustrated by Yoshiko Jaeggi. Art © 2008 by Yoshiko Jaeggi. Permission to reprint granted by Peachtree Publishers.

Figure 3.1 (page 57): From *Yatandou* by Gloria Whelan. Illustrated by Peter Sylvada. Used with permission from Sleeping Bear Press, a Cengage Learning company.

Figure 3.2 (page 61): From *Buster* by Denise Fleming. Illustrated by Denise Fleming. Illustration copyright © 2003 by Denise Fleming. Reprinted by permission of Henry Holt and Company, LLC.

Figure 4.1 (page 80): From *The Butter Man* by Elizabeth Alalou and Ali Alalou. Illustrated by Julie Klear Essakalli. Illustration copyright © 2008 by Julie Klear Essakalli. All rights reserved, including the right of reproduction in whole or in part in any form. Used with permission by Charlesbridge Publishing, Inc.

Figure 4.2 (pages 94–95): From *Ziba Came on a Boat* by Liz Lofthouse. Ilustrated by Robert Ingpen. Illustration © 2007. Reprinted by permission of Kane Miller, a Division of EDC Publishing, Tulsa, OK.

Figure 4.3 (page 97): From *Thank You World* by Alice McGinty. Illustrated by Wendy Anderson Halperin. Text © 2007 by Alice B. McGinty. Illustration ©2007 by Wendy Anderson Halperin. Used by permission of Dial Books for Young Readers, a division of Penguin Young Readers Group, a member of Penguin Group (USA) Inc., 345 Hudson Street, New York, NY 10014. All rights reserved.

Figure 5.1 (pages 114–115): From *Whoosh Went the Wind* by Sally Derby. Illustrated by Vincent Nguyen. Illustration copyright © 2006 by Vincent Nguyen. Reproduced by permission of the publisher, Marshall Cavendish, 99 White Plains Road, Tarrytown, NY 10591.

Figure 5.2 (page 133): From *Moongirl* by Henry Selick. Illustrated by Peter Chan and Courtney Booker. Copyright © 2006 by Laika Entertainment. Reproduced by permission of the publisher, Candlewick Press, Somerville, MA.

Figure 6.1 (page 142): From *The Three Snow Bears* by Jan Brett. Illustrated by Jan Brett. Illustration copyright ©2007 by Jan Brett. Used by permission of G. P. Putnam's Sons, a division of Penguin Young Readers Group, a member of Penguin Group (USA) Inc., 345 Hudson Street, New York, NY 10014. All rights reserved.

Figure 6.2 (page 146): From *The Ghost Catcher: A Bengali Folktale* by Martha Hamilton and Mitch Weiss. Illustrated by Kristen Balouch. Illustration copyright © 2008 by Kristen Balouch. Published by August House, Inc., Atlanta, GA.

Figure 6.3 (page 148): From *Dick Whittington and His Cat* retold by Margaret Hodges. Illustrated by Mélisande Potter. Illustration copyright © 2006 by Mélisande Potter. All rights reserved. Reprinted by permission of Holiday House, Inc.

Index

Page numbers in bold indicate annotations. Page numbers in italic indicate illustrations.

Index

Index

Index

Index